Lessons for the Little Boy

A Man's Conversation with His Younger Self

A Reflective Journey to Manhood

Cover Design: Destiny Darcel
Manuascript Editor: Amy Rothblatt
Interior Design: Janie Lee
Published by: 220 Publishing

Lessons for the Little Boy: A Man's Conversation to His Younger Self
A Reflective Journey to Manhood. Jaime A. Gill. First Edition.
ISBN: 978-1-5136-8859-6

Featuring

Jaime A. Gill

Jim Smith

Willow James

Glenn Murray

Freddie B. Arnold, Jr.

Bishop Kevin Whitaker

Peyton Rose

Shawn Mason

Eric Hampton

Kenery Smith

Lionel Hilaire

Mel Roberson

Robert Hazzard, Jr.

Carlo Kennedy

This book is dedicated to:

1. The men that raised me who are now my guardian angels:
   My Father, Alton R. Gill
   Grandfathers: James A. Smith Sr., Mack Gill and Otis P. Harris
   God Father, Charles Golden Sr.

   Thank you for loving me, protecting me, fiercely supporting me and teaching me every moment of my life—until your very last breaths.

2. My brothers, Patrick Gill and Tony Muhammad

   Thank you for always making me feel special and like the most important person in your world, whenever we shared time together.

3. My nephews: Sherman Jr, Donta Vaughn, Tony Gill Jr, Rasul Muhammad, Ezekiel Muhammad, Keith Jones, and Phillip Jones.

   May each of you continue to learn and grow to be men that you admire and that leaves a positive impact wherever you are. May faith, hope, and strength be with you always.

A special thank you to Floyd Wilson for lighting the spark for this book to be written. God used you in such a fabulous way to show me that there was more! Continued blessings, favor and peace to you always!

TABLE OF CONTENTS

WELCOME LETTER   6
Jaime A. Gill

FOREWORD   8
Jim Smith

THE HEART OF A MAN   10
by Jaime A. Gill

FOR THE BOYS   12
by Willow James

LESSONS TO MY YOUNGER SELF   14
by Glenn Murray

THE MENTAL BATTLE: A FATHER'S PERSPECTIVE   22
By Freddie B. Arnold Jr.

FAITH IT TIL YOU MAKE IT   25
Bishop Kevin Whitaker

THE SILENT TEACHER   31
By Peyton Rose

YOUNG, GIFTED, AND...   39
By Shawn Mason

RUN YOUR RACE   43
By Eric Hampton

LEARN TO PLAY TO JAZZ   46
By Kenery Kent Smith

THE LIFE-LONG JOURNEY   49
By Lionel Hilaire

FATHER FIGURE   55
By Mel Roberson

FAMILY MATTERS   59
By Robert Hazzard, Jr.

THE LESSONS CONTINUE   62
By Carlo Kennedy

Greetings Gentlemen,

I am so excited that you are here. I would like to tell you how this book became a reality that is now in your hands.

This book, *Lessons for the Little Boy,* is a sequel to my book, *Lessons for the Little Girl: Lessons to Learn, to Live, and to Love,* which was released in 2014.

Lessons for the Little Girl was created to invite women and girls to embark on the process of self-reflection, through journaling and reflecting on experiences in their own lives, while reading about experiences from my childhood. The book has reached international borders and has empowered hundreds of women, one "little girl" at a time.

In October of 2014, I had the honor of being a vendor at a comedy show, where I sold my newly released book, *Lessons for The Little Girl.* There were quite a few men that came there to purchase the book. I asked whoever purchased the book if they wanted me to sign it and address it to a particular woman/girl in their life. One man stated boldly, "THIS IS FOR ME." He continued by saying, "If you have something good for women, I am sure you have something a man can learn, too."

It was at that moment that the dream of Lessons for the Little Boy began. It became overwhelmingly evident that the opportunity that I created in the book for women and girls to reflect was also needed for men and boys. Self-reflection is not EXCLUSIVE... it's inclusive. What is good for the goose is good for the gander in this respect. Moreover, self-reflection on both sides allows relationships to be stronger-and I am learning that you become less dependent on someone else to make you "whole." You begin to realize that you, as an individual, are complete. Even though you may have some imperfections, you are still a vessel that is full of value and abilities. I desire this book to be a platform for men to have a conversation with each other: sharing advice, wisdom, mistakes, and experiences with each other, and the younger ones watching, learning, and gleaning information.

Men, this book is my gift to you. Your mental, emotional, spiritual, and physical well-being matters to me, because I am a daughter, granddaughter, niece, aunt, sister, friend, neighbor, and co-worker... your presence impacts my presence. So, may you PRESENT the best version of yourself through the journey of self-reflection.

The men that are the contributing authors of this book will be your guides through self-reflection. They were specifically chosen for you.I believe that these men offer wisdom and perspective that is encouraging to all, despite age, race, culture, economic, or political positioning.

Before I leave you men to have your sacred space, I want to share an experience I had with my father, which was further confirmation that this book was needed. Through the featured authors' words, and your reflections on them, may you be positioned to give the best version of yourself to the world.

I love you. I appreciate you. I support you. I am grateful for your existence. I believe in you! Enjoy your journey!

— *Jaime A. Gill, Visionary Author*

When my niece Jaime asked me to write the foreword for this book, I must admit I was surprised and honored. Many thoughts crossed my mind about what I could share. Now that I am in my 60's, I realize I have experienced and learned a lot.

I was reared in Robbins, a small, tight-knit community in a suburb of Chicago. The men and women in my family were impeccable examples of strength and fortitude. After graduating from the University of Michigan, I knew that the process of maturing from a boy to a man was truly beginning.

As a student athlete in college, I participated in one of the greatest college football programs in the country, which required a lot of focus and responsibility. After graduation I had the opportunity to play professional football for ten seasons, before moving on to other life and career goals.

Now, as a man, husband, and the father of five wonderful and profoundly unique sons, a grandfather to a beautiful granddaughter, a brother, an uncle, a businessman, and a coach,

I realize how many roles I fill on any given day.

There is a famous quote in the play King Henry the Fourth by William Shakespeare that says, "uneasy is the head that wears the crown." It is often translated as, "heavy is the head that wears the crown." This statement, in many respects, speaks to the weight of responsibility that is given to a king or a leader. I can identify with the sentiment of this statement deeply, as I strive to be the best man that I can be. I know that having the support of my family, my faith, and my ability to do healthy introspection, is what helps me persevere.

As I think about what I could offer to you, I think about my sons and what I hope for them as young men growing up in a world that is vastly different from the one that I grew up in. No matter how much things may change around you, knowing who you are is the key to survival. Self-reflection has acted as my North Star. Very early in life, I was taught to be honest with myself and ask myself very hard questions:

- Where am I?
- What is my goal/agenda?
- Am I working towards that goal/agenda?
- What is preventing me from the achievement of that goal/agenda?
- Am I willing to pay the price to get there?
- Is it worth it?

I have found these questions to be true in just about all aspects of my life: personal relationships, educationally, spiritually, and from a business perspective. You may have a different set of questions. What this book and the contributing authors desire to do is to present you with the opportunity to not only develop your own questions, but to put you on the path to FINDING YOUR ANSWERS!

Know that your crown was made specifically for you. Wear it well, Gentlemen!

Best Wishes,
Jim Smith

THE HEART OF THE MAN
by Jaime A. Gill

One day, in my junior year of college, I was sitting in the car with my father after church. I did not see my father very much growing up, so, as a young adult, I was determined to spend more time with him to strengthen our relationship. I loved my daddy, and I knew my daddy loved me, but I didn't want it to be just because we were father and daughter. I wanted us to know each other as individuals. I wanted him to know my favorite things, and I wanted to know what brought him joy. I wanted us to know what our fears were and what brought us pain. So, on this particular day, my father and I sat sharing some of those things. I had imagined this day in my head many times, but I never anticipated that my response would be what it was.

As my father began to express some of his truths, I became angry. This shocked me. So, as he shared his pain with me, my immediate response to his pain was to share mine. And, in the car on that Sunday afternoon, I had my first highly emotional conversation with my father. There were raised voices, there were tears, there was confusion, and much frustration.

What I have begun to realize was that I was not being fair to my father that day. I opened the door and asked him to come in emotionally. Then, in essence, I was rejecting and, I hate to admit it, ridiculing him for coming into the very place that I had invited him. It takes courage to be vulnerable—especially in front of others, and I think even more so for parents to be vulnerable to their children; specifically, a father to his daughter. And maybe being vulnerable is just difficult for a man in general.

Men are often viewed as being strong and unemotional, or at least limited emotionally. They don't seem to have weak moments, especially in front of someone… or do they? Maybe that's the entire point of it all. Moreover, women's expectations of what a man should be, and how he should behave, have often hindered more relationships than helped them. I didn't want to love my daddy for who I thought he was, or who I wanted him to be. I wanted to love my daddy for who he actually was—because of and in spite of it.

This was the first moment that led to many more moments of me learning about my daddy and hearing not only his words, but his heart. I discovered that, as a man, my daddy had deep scars from childhood that were not entirely healed. He had developed more scars as a man that, in turn, reminded him of the unhealed scars of his childhood. And my daddy did his best to move past them, or not deal with them, so that he could "BE A MAN." But based on whose definition?

As my dad grew older, I began to see how he didn't fight to convince people of who he was—he just was! And, as my father got closer to the end of his life, I saw how he made peace with the things that he had done, and maybe had not done. As my sister and I watched our father take his last breath on August 2, 2019, two days after my 40th birthday, I knew that my dad was able to leave this earth knowing that he tried his best, and that he was the best man he knew how to be. And I had peace because I had taken the opportunity to learn to know the man, to love the man. And that is the man I miss.

FOR THE BOYS
by Willow James

This one is for the boys. The boys just learning how to speak. The middle child boy. The boys who just reached double digits. The boys waiting in line at the DMV. The boys in college. The boys who are boys, regardless of what others say. The boys who were told not to cry. The boys purchasing their first crib, and for their little boys. The boys who like other boys. The boys who aren't able in one way but are able in others. The big boys, the men. The men who've made it over the hill. The men with a little gray. The men who can tell you about back in the day. This is for all of you. And for me.

From my experience, one cannot be taught to "be a boy." There isn't a guide or a manual. No podcasts or documentaries to help. Throughout your life, others may tell you what boys do or don't do. "Boys will be boys," they'll say. They may advise you to "man up," but don't you worry about what it means because chances are the person who said it doesn't know either.

Lucky for you, I've been a boy for a while now and picked up some stuff along the way. Ready?

1. Like what you like. Like who you like. In all ways.

2. Listen to yourself. Listen to others the same way you'd want them to listen to you.

3. Cry if you feel like it because "holding it all in" isn't the best practice. You can't keep pouring water into a cup and not expect it to overflow.

4. Boyhood never stops. It only evolves. As you venture through

manhood, never stop playing and getting lost in your imagination.

5. You are special, but you aren't the most important person in the world.

6. Don't be tough. Sometimes you will not be okay. That's okay.

7. Respect, appreciate, and honor the girls and women in your life. And the ones not in your life.

8. You can do anything you really want to do, for good or for evil. Be careful.

9. Reread numbers one through eight. You may be told that the opposite is true for each one of them. Don't fall for it. Trust me on this!

Most importantly, show the other boys you meet in life how it's done. History will thank you for it.

I wish you joy, growth, and everlasting boyhood.

Sincerely,
Just Another Boy

LESSONS TO MY YOUNGER SELF
by Glenn Murray

A few months before initially sitting down to write this, I was interviewed for a show by Jamila Thomas, based in Dallas, TX. She asked me a question that would become the inspiration for everything you're about to read.

"If you could sit down with your younger self, what advice would you give yourself?"

I thought, "What a great question, but where would I start?" A conversation with my 25-30 years younger self. What lessons, reflections, and, most importantly, "warnings" would I share with younger Glenn? The part that I feared most was how much of myself, my thoughts, my failures would I share? This was beyond just a conversation with myself; this was for the world to see. I've always encouraged others to open their lives through their writing. To "change the world" and "find their purpose," among other grandiose statements. But, in pushing others forward, they provided perfect cover for the flawed person that was lying just beneath an "exterior" that I worked hard to keep polished. Was I going to take my own advice? After much deliberation, here for all the world to see, are the lessons for the little boy who, in so many ways, still lives in me.

LIVE WITHOUT FEAR

When I look at my younger self, let's say I'm 16, I was still very much in an awkward state, not quite figuring out what in the world to do. Living fearlessly was still many years away. Confidence is often the last trait we inherit because the feelings of inadequacy, and worrying about others and what they think, are often top of mind. Live fearlessly. Learn that, as you grow older, slowly but surely your creativity drifts away. Responsibilities increase with each year we add to our lives. There's the "free-wheeling 20s," the "more concerned about stability 30s," and the "security and future-focused 40s." Each decade takes a little of the "edge" off, and we try to capture bits and pieces of it. But life works hard to take that fearlessness away, that feeling that you're free to do anything, be anything, go anywhere. That feeling of wonder, of anticipation that we feel only when the world is in front of us. That's what I would tell my younger self—don't lose that feeling. Every day you're alive the world is in front of you. Wake up each day hoping to make it better than the one before it. However, life will get in the way.

In your 20s, you won't have enough money, in your 30s, you'll have to work too much, and in your 40s, you won't want to take many chances. LIVE! The world will open up to you if you open yourself up to the world. There are 80-year-olds getting college degrees, skydiving, and traveling the world. What's your excuse if you're half their age? Imagine you're 16 again... what would you do over? Where were you planning on traveling when you reached adulthood? What did you say you were going to do but never did? There is a list of "I wanted to" and "I should haves." Never lose that spirit of wonder and adventure that we possessed in our youth. You're only as young as you feel.

In my 40s I've been able to travel, build businesses, and experience life through a very different lens. I wish I could say there weren't mistakes made, too much money spent, too much time chasing the wrong things (and the wrong people.) But I needed to live through the bumps and bruises to get to my "better."

LOSS

As a child, I remember accompanying my grandmother to see friends who were ill: lifelong friends, church members, and neighbors. It was her, representing the Murray family, doing her part to let people know that their friendship meant something. The visits were always joyful reminiscing about good times, bringing food or just sitting quietly, which I could never do easily as a child, but tried. I think that's why I learned so much patience at an early age—observing and spending so much time with those older than me. I often think about those times now when checking on friends.

Today there are so many ways to "check in" versus when I was growing up. A text, a Facebook note, or an email have all become acceptable. While some still require the good old phone call, the point is that communication is now easier than it has ever been. If I could give my younger self advice it would be to value those friendships.There are friends you'll make at twelve that you'll have all your life.Cherish those relationships, you'll meet many more throughout the years; some will come, some will go. Those that stay—let them know that you appreciate them. Inevitably some will pass from this world way before their time.

The unfortunate fact about growing up in this day and age is that we live in a time of the increasing societal impact of violence, illness, and disease. Almost everyone my age knows someone who died prematurely. It has become a natural part of your life and an uncomfortable truth, making the value of each relationship all the more important. You need to know that you will lose friends to cancer, to gun violence, to AIDs, to preventable illnesses, diabetes, and recently, to COVID-19. You need to know that you'll spend countless hours wondering why. What made him be the one to outlast those friends lost?What was the purpose? You'll question God when, in a span of 24 months, three of your closest friends will die at the age of 40 from cancer, 43 from un-detected type 2 diabetes, and from lupus at 45. And sometimes you'll even lash out in anger and ignorance in a flurry of emotion. Know that, while being strong for friends and for those left, you'll spend many nights crying about the loss, and that it's all acceptable and normal. Then, just as the pain starts to subside, you'll suffer the greatest loss, the loss of your best friend: your mother.

Nothing prepares you for that and nothing will ever be the same in your life: the way you look at the world, the fear of losing the person who always had your best interests at heart. You'll need to be strong as cancer ravages her body, you'll leave your job to spend the last six months of her life close by her side. You'll learn more about emergency rooms, treatments, procedures, and all things cancer than you'll ever want to. The person who was with you when you took your first breath, you'll be there when she takes her last. And again, you'll be angry with God. You'll ask why, when she spent every day of her illness believing He'd heal her. Never wavering, always faithful. But He didn't save her; not in the way you wanted, and the way she believed He would. And you'll question Him again and again and you'll never get a direct answer. You'll go through depression, and you won't tell anyone. You'll fight it by throwing yourself into work and your social life.But you won't heal yourself by doing any of that.

You'll learn to search deep within yourself, and start to cultivate all those lessons from mom, from dad, from friends. You'll learn that you must grow your purpose from the fertile soil that holds your pain.You'll learn, as we all do, that life is a blessing that comes with an expiration date. Those close to you are a blessing, and loss becomes an ongoing reminder of just how fleeting that blessing is.

There will be more people lost over the years after this—suddenly without warning, and then there will be the pandemic losses: the mothers, the fathers, the friends. And, again, you'll ask yourself why. The difference is that you'll never take anyone for granted. Your strength will help others who have to learn to grow through their pain.I wish it was easy, but purpose never is. You'll learn that, as a man, you have emotions, and that there are times in life when those emotions weigh so heavy on your heart-and that's ok. Hurt is not reserved for any specific group. You hurt to enable others to heal. You'll feel alone, but you really aren't. Eventually there will be daylight: a period when the pain and darkness of the loss will dissipate, and you'll look back on the loss, and the "little boy" will finally understand that life seems endless, and that friendships will last forever when we're young. But, although youth is just a mirage for the sting of reality, it's only the possibilities of your life that are truly endless.

FAMILY

What can you say about family? You're born with them. As we grow up, they are usually put there to annoy us... we think. (This was especially true about some of my cousins.) I grew up as my mother's only child. That meant spending lots of time alone and spending lots of time with people older than me.

I have a wonderful family as well, including brothers and sisters that are amazing people. But I grew up, until the age of 14, thinking that it was only me. I met those brothers and sisters later in life and, through the years, I've come to spend time with them and love them as if we grew up in a traditional two-parent household. I would say that "family" is a term that can be loosely used to describe close friends as well as blood relatives. You start building your family early from a group of friends and relatives. You grow up and grow together and sometimes apart, but you have the ability to make them your family.

You'll get a long lesson on understanding fatherhood and what it means to be a father, a lesson you won't fully understand until your 40s. Even if you grow up mainly without a father, you will understand and respect the journey. So many women must take on the task of raising boys alone to be upstanding men. You'll be very confused about your relationship with your father well into your 30s, but you should not allow that to be an excuse for not becoming the man you need to become.

It takes a man to admit his faults and work on improving every day of his life. You'll learn to love and respect your father for that reason and love your mother even more for being able to raise you with that understanding. There will be many who will never come to that revelation, and you may be one of them, but your start will never determine your finish.

There are many of us who still have that angry little boy inside them about a parental relationship. You will mature for the good of family relationships, and your own reconciliation of those relationships.I wish I could tell you that the family would turn out to be one big picture of happiness. But that simply isn't the truth. However, you are responsible for how you respond and nurture those relationships.Make the most of your family. Forgive, forget, move forward, and respect each other and you'll have done your part.

LOVE AND RELATIONSHIPS

When I first thought about writing my "lessons," this is the subject I'm probably least qualified to give advice on. There are days, although "good and grown," I still struggle to understand the dynamics of this topic. There is a song by Pat Benatar titled, "Love Is a Battlefield." I believe it's more like a minefield, and men seem to step on every mine imaginable while trying to navigate. You'll need to remember the following things:

1. There are people that will love you no matter what you do. Be careful to respect them and their feelings, even if you don't feel the same way.

2. You are going to do the wrong thing and break somebody's heart.I wish I could tell you that you won't, but you will, and you'll do it more than once.

3. You'll learn that everyone who loves you doesn't have your best interests at heart. Love can be a very selfish emotion that isolates one's thinking (you only understand this when you've actually fallen in love, and you will.)

4. You will have your heart broken. You won't forget it because, as a man, you'll try to avoid it with all your being, and then, when you can't, it's such a foreign feeling that you won't understand why it happened and what she could be thinking!There will be at least one, maybe more. Don't dwell on the one that got away; look forward to the one who will eventually stay.

5. If you treat those that you choose to be in a relationship with like they are special and with respect, if it comes to an end,

you will actually help them take more than heartbreak from a relationship if it doesn't work out. And yes, they may even consider you a friend down the road (that road may be long and don't expect miracles!)

6. Not everyone is equipped to love you like you want and deserve. Conversely, you aren't always equipped to love someone like they want and deserve. Timing is everything!

7. It's OK to apologize. You'll mess up (I can't stress that enough!) and sometimes that apology won't be accepted. But you absolutely should do it.

8. Don't be afraid (easier said than done, I know), but remember the first lesson: if you learn to love without fear, you will be able to experience life in a whole new way-with someone by your side.

I wish I had someone to tell me this when I was younger.Love is often the hardest lesson for a man to learn because we are process driven; we think it happens when we activate a switch. If we could package it into something men could understand, like a football game, things would be much easier. 1st quarter you meet her, 2nd quarter you begin to date seriously, halftime you look at your options, realize she's the best and the game plan is to keep her. 3rd quarter you start your offensive to keep her and make her feel special. 4th quarter you shut it all down and make her yours forever.

The problem is that men tend to linger in "halftime" a little too long to suit women. I would let my younger self know that he's going to spend his 20's in halftime, and his 30's trying to correct his mistakes by throwing "Hail Mary" passes (a desperation pass to score a touchdown, for the non-football educated.) You need to have your head in the entire game; you can't change your game in the 4th quarter and expect to win the person you actually want. Love, like life, needs to be experienced without regrets. And sometimes the one that got away won't come back. Take that lesson and cherish the one that eventually stays.

MAKE A LIST

Make a list of the things you want to do-then it becomes real. Make a list of the places you want to go. (You're going to love Paris, by the way! And you're going to spend way too much time in Vegas... but you'll enjoy every moment of it.) Make a list of the ways you can serve others. Make a list of the ways, when you find that special one, you'll make sure they never leave. Make a list of the friends and family you need to routinely check on. Tell people you love them. Tell people you're proud of them. Live without fear. Love without condition. Never forget those you've lost. Love yourself. Respect yourself and respect others. Serve and learn your purpose and become the man I know you can be.

THE MENTAL BATTLE: A FATHER'S PERSPECTIVE

By Freddie B. Arnold Jr.

The alarm clock sounds at 5:30 AM. I lay in the bed for 30 minutes, mentally preparing to depart the confines of my home to embark upon an "imperfect trifecta," which is a job, a city, and a world—none of which care about my mental wellness, my ambitions, or family. An "Imperfect Trifecta" that sees a man prepared to face any obstacle that may confront him throughout the day, a man that will need to rapidly respond to a day full of finding solutions to problems that may occur.

As I continue to lie here at daybreak, I am psychologically clothing myself with the armor of God preparing for today's earthly battle: the world outside, compared to the comfort of my home. A world without the beautiful smiles and melodious voices of the four women—my wife and three girls, that I will not hear or see for the next 13-14 hours, until I return home.

It's 6:00 AM now, I rise from my bed to start my preparation for the day, but my thoughts are still revolving. Now I'm unconsciously thinking about the ladies in my house. This time it is not about my battle, it's about theirs, the four women in my house: more specifically, about my three daughters. Are they prepared?

Men are taught in their adolescent years to be masculine and prepared for tribulation. We are introduced to these characteristics through sports, communications, bodily gestures, and or behaviors, leaving no doubt about their manhood. He should be courageous, strong physically, and mentally agile. Men should show no weakness and should display little to no emotions. These are rites of passage that have been passed down from fathers to sons for generations.

As a father of three girls, I, too, exhibited all the characteristics of manhood, passing down to them what was taught to me. But I quickly identified that, unlike raising young men, showing little to no emotions was not part of the "Daddy Program" for girls. Oh no. After the first cry, first smile, and first hug from my daughters—any one of them, my heart was stolen. I had to approach raising daughters a little differently, as it was obvious that I was emotionally immature. I consistently attempted to remain steadfast in my tough mentality but had failed miserably.

Immediately, I transitioned to becoming more nurturing, loving, and affectionate much sooner than if I had been raising a son. Now, this is not to say that young men do not need the same parenting techniques; but, put simply, the approach to displaying affection is significantly different. In fatherhood, we have the responsibility of helping our children develop the ability to face whatever obstacles may come their way, but the fork in the road splits with girls and boys at that tween age, that age between 9 and 12 years old. In this age range, the emotional gender gap becomes more apparent, and different life applications based on these genders are required for their future development.

At 6:00 AM I am still pondering... Have I prepared my daughters, as I have prepared myself, to enter the "Imperfect Trifecta?" See, my thoughts are not about whether I have equipped them to be strategic in their careers, independent thinkers, and/or financially independent. Rather, my thoughts are centered around the choices they would make when they enter the workforce and are faced with harassment. My thoughts are centered about whether they are comfortable within their skin and their bodies, as the world constantly displays what they think a woman's appearance should look like. My thoughts are, are they able to identify and protect themselves from the dangers in the world that prey on women? I do not want my 6:00 AM thoughts to become gender biased, but they are, for I am raising three young women that will face obstacles that many men will not face.

Women over the last several decades have made tremendous contributions in the corporate and political sectors of the world. They have catapulted into positions of leadership that men once controlled, but in doing so, they have sacrificed so much. They have either forfeited their chances of having children, or postponed a long-standing relationship, and/or familial stability. Those that have families are often forced to choose work over family and, when choosing family, they are identified as being meek, weak, or are met with disapproval and a glass ceiling for advancement. This is the reason that I worry. I envision my daughters with loving families and career choices that support their life's purposes, without having to sacrifice their morals and goals. I envision their entrepreneurial spirits to not be hindered because they embrace their natural beauty (hair, facial features, body, etc.), unlike the image of what the media has portrayed how a successful African American woman should look in today's society. Have I prepared them?

The time is now 7:15 AM. As I depart from the confines and safety of my home, I remind my wife in a soft voice that I love her. I am ready to battle the trifecta; yet my daughters are still constantly on my mind. I am convinced that this will never end, for I have so much I need to teach them, but I know that I can only teach them so much about life. As I have learned, and so will they, life is learning through daily life applications. A father's love for his children will never end, but a daughter's overbearing, protective father's love will always have him questioning, "Are they prepared?"

FAITH IT TIL YOU MAKE IT

By Bishop Kevin Whitaker

When I was asked to participate in this amazing project, I thought it would be easy to write, but then I realized I had so many lessons that I wanted to share that it was a difficult task narrowing them down! Then, there is the question of how far back did I dare go? So, I began to ponder, and I remembered that, even as a young boy when we lived on the south side of Chicago, I was a dreamer—I mean, I had a very expansive imagination.

I'm thinking it was in 1977 when the new Spiderman toy was introduced, and there was a piece you could attach to your wrist, which dispensed an artificial web. And I remember watching Spiderman and I believe that that's when my dreaming began! Imagine this: I stood on the 3rd floor of an apartment building, my heart is racing, my thoughts are scattered, and I'm looking at my new Spiderman web dispenser. I'm staring out the window, and thinking to myself that, if this works for Spiderman, surely it can work for me.

I am approximately eight feet from the other building and all I'm thinking is, "if I shoot my web, I can swing downstairs and hang with my friends!" My heart is racing and I'm sweating and thinking, "Go for it Kevin!!!" I raised the window and looked down, and then I became afraid to fall, and thank God Spiderman was not real—you can't really swing from a web. However, as make-believe as Spiderman is, the ability to jump and to navigate around obstacles is something that needs to be applied in real life: shoot your web and swing into purpose and destiny!!

So, I would tell my younger self many things like, "always dream, and if that doesn't work out, dream bigger, because you have a destiny and a purpose that's already been prearranged and all you have to do is to stay focused." Staying focused is critical, because, growing up in the hood or the ghetto, it's easy to lose focus due to all of the things that we have allowed to become normal that had really traumatized us: like the single-parent homes, the crime, the drugs, the poverty, and the lack of opportunity that I'm certain is not everyone's experience, but it's the experience of many of us and, no matter how normal it has become, this just shouldn't be.

When we began to look biblically at the lives of many, we will see from David all the way to John, and we see that they were who they were before becoming fully manifested! When we look at the life of David the Worshipping warrior, ultimately having too much blood on his hands to build God a temple, we see from the beginning, before he killed Goliath, that he had already killed a lion and a bear: it was already in him!!!

We must note that, whatever we are to become, the seed for it is already there, and over the years we water that seed and cause it to grow!! Some of us water it with agony and suffering, trials and tribulations, and, whatever we have to do to become, that's what we'll do!! Because it's already in us.

When we look at the dreamer Joseph, we understand that his brothers couldn't handle his dreams because his dreams detailed an outcome that was favorable to Joseph. So, he is then betrayed by his brothers and sold into slavery. Yet, The Bible declares that the Lord was with him-so much so that Potiphar saw it and allowed him to RISE TO POWER! And, when he looked back at his journey too many times, having encountered many trials and tribulations that began with the initial betrayal of his brothers, he understands the providence of God and that what you intended to be declared evil, God meant to be for my good in a time such as this! Because the plan of God will always overthrow the plan of the wicked! It was already in him! Then, I would say that staying focused is more than a notion. I would encourage my younger self to look and live beyond the limitations that surround him because, even though he's built for it, he's also built by it! I would tell him to seek the will of God.

I must admit that this is a bit of a mystery to most, simply because we would all like to think that we know what this is for us and for those we love. We sometimes believe that the Will of God places us on a bed of ease, and that anything difficult would automatically point us in another direction contrary to the struggle. One of the things we must understand about the Will of God is that it will often come with challenges, it will often come with resistance, and we must be able to navigate through tough times, in order to reach our goals.

When traveling in a car, you may come to some bumps in the road. However, you just take your time to cross over bumps, so you won't damage the vehicle. Likewise in life: sometimes bumps will slow you down and you may have to take your time in order to get through that bumpy situation, which you need to understand. And even though it takes a little longer, you don't want to rush because, if you speed over the bumpy roads, you may become damaged and never reach your destiny.

Now, something else can happen as you are attempting to reach your destiny. You can program your navigation and it will give you the best route, the fastest and most common route, but you may come to a detour and, once you come to that detour, you will have to take an alternate route. It may not be as quick, it may not be the most popular, however, it's the best route at that moment for you to travel!!! So, don't be afraid of alternate routes.

Let me explain, using a scene from the popular television show, "The Fresh Prince of Bel-Air." This scene has Will Smith in a class that he didn't like, so he did everything he could to get dismissed from it. Once he was removed from the class, he was walking by the classroom only to discover that he didn't like the class at all; rather, he loved it, and that it would be essential to his life and where he was going. So, he asked to be put back in the class, then finds out that the class is full, and that the only way he could take the class was to take it without receiving credit from the school, but he would get what he needed for his life. Therefore, often the alternate route may take longer, it may cost you, and you may not get recognized for it-but if you do what is necessary, there will be a lasting reward.

Now, since I'm proving my point by using travel terminology and, while I'm writing this, I'm on a plane, it's only befitting that I use this analogy. While flying in a plane, you can experience all sorts of situations—from your takeoff to your landing, and there are many revelations you may come to that will assist you in your journey.

When a plane is taking off, it uses the most fuel because it takes a lot to lift a machine of this magnitude, as you are moving towards your destiny. You have goals and direction and passion and all the things you need, in order to arrive at a certain place in life: starting with the takeoff, or the beginning of your journey. There may be clouds and wind and maybe even rain. All of these can produce quite a bit of turbulence, and can make the ride bumpy, uncomfortable, and maybe even make you fearful.

I liken this to things we may encounter on our journey-whether it be heartbreak, disappointment, betrayal, or all of it, and the reality is that you cannot, and will not, live in this life and deal with human beings without experiencing pain by encountering people. It's an inevitable rite of passage, an initiation of sorts, into Life's journey towards success, and just as a plane has to, at times, rise above the clouds, rise above the winds, rise above the rain, in order to continue moving forward, likewise you must rise. You will never see or hear a pilot get angry because of the turbulence-he just rises above it, and if turbulence exists at the place where the plane has maximized its lift, then you just Buckle up for the ride!!! Because life at every level can bring about turbulence, from the beginning to the epitome of success, and there will be many instances when turbulence will present itself.

Now here's something that's interesting because, as the plane is taking off, it needs to build up great speed in order to lift the plane, and you can feel and see that you're moving fast! However, when you are up in the air, it appears that you're not moving that fast at all, but, in actuality, you're now moving much faster so the question becomes, why does it appear that I'm moving slowly? It's because the higher up I am, the more ground I cover, so it gives the appearance that I'm moving slowly, but I'm moving fast and arriving at my destiny. Can I submit to you that you're up high and you're covering ground, and that God has you right where you need to be in order to execute... so execute!

Back to the essence of this lesson, which is to seek the Will of God. What does that really mean? Let's see and let's define "will."

Will:
1. used to express desire, choice, willingness, consent
2. used to express frequent, customary, or habitual behavior it means to desire or even wish!

So that, according to Webster, we must seek or attempt to discover what God's choice is for us. Webster's dictionary definition also delves into God's intentions for us, which, through the Prophet Jeremiah, reveals what the will of God, or the intention of God, is for his life before he was even born! "Before I formed thee in the belly, I knew thee; and before thou camest forth out of the womb, I sanctified thee, and I ordained thee a prophet unto the nations." (Jeremiah 1:5.) So here we see that the Will of God for Jeremiah was already in place before he was even born into this world, which speaks to a prearranged, inevitable plan for his life.

I firmly believe that, as we come into this world, there are paths that have been prepared for us to take, and that, in the beginning of our lives, we spend a good amount of time trying to see why we are here; and, as a matter of fact, some people live their whole lives without ever knowing what role the Will of God will play during the course of their lifetimes.

Then, later in the book of Jeremiah, he further states that, "I know the thoughts that I have towards you, they are thoughts of good and not evil to bring you to an expected end." (Jeremiah 29:11.)

God is informing us here that his intentions are good. Now the problem is that, although knowing God has good intentions, that doesn't always eliminate the fear or anxiety about what not always having the tangible proof of what your life is going to become.

Perhaps one of the most insightful statements I'll make is this: you've always been on the path of becoming. "THAT'S RIGHT, YOU'VE ALWAYS BEEN EVOLVING INTO THE FULLNESS OF WHO YOU WILL COMPLETELY BECOME."

When there is no tangible proof of who you are becoming, and no outward indication of my evolution, it becomes hard; yet, again, stay the course and ultimately, you'll get there.

Looking at my life and, even though I'm not where I want to be, I've accomplished many things and have been places that I'd never thought I'd go. So, I say to you, learn from every phase of life, persevere through every tough time, know you have what it takes and that there is an ultimate plan for your life!

THE SILENT TEACHER
By Peyton Rose

I grew up in a little town in Arkansas. My family didn't have much. We were poor and my father wasn't around very often. I realized, very early on, that if I wanted something, I would need to find a way to get it myself. My home life was not pleasant. As a matter of fact, it was pretty scary. I never knew when my father would come home and what he would be like when he did. He had severe problems with drugs and alcohol, and he took out his anger on me. This fueled my own rage, and I often acted out in wild and unruly ways.

I learned that voicing my opinion, or asking for help, would be met with animosity, and often physical or mental abuse from my dad. This made me even more angry and resentful. I resented my father. I resented people around me, other kids who looked like they had perfect lives. I even resented the kids who had tough lives like mine.

I was told, "You are a mistake. You are cursed to fail." I was told that the world was a hard place, and that people would take advantage of me anytime they had a chance. And, for some time I believed it. I resented the whole world. I was mad at everything, and my performance at school was a reflection of this anger.

Then, one day something changed in me. I was in the third grade and my class was watching a movie about a little girl named Helen Keller. Like me, she was born in a small town in the South.

When Helen was 19 months old, she became deaf and blind, due to an unknown illness—perhaps rubella or scarlet fever. As she got older, she became wild and unruly.

Helen spent the early days of her life not knowing how to speak or write; she didn't even know what words were.

There was a teacher named Anne Sullivan who took an interest in Helen. She wanted to help the little girl learn about words and how to use them. So, she began teaching Helen. She started with one word-the word: "doll." Anne had taken an interest in Helen, and Helen now took an interest in words. Soon she had mastered the entire alphabet. And soon after that she was learning 30 words a day! Helen dedicated her life to learning, and she proved to be an amazing student.

Helen Keller went on to become one of the most talented writers of her time, and she is still recognized as one of the most inspiring writers who has ever lived.

Something awakened within me on the day that I learned about Helen Keller. Here was a girl who couldn't hear or speak, and she went on to be one of the most celebrated authors ever. She overcame a challenge that I could never imagine. Her story gave me new hope. I was inspired like I never was before. I realized that, as long as I had my mind, I could do anything. No matter what my father did to me-if he beat me up, if he called me names and told me I was worthless, it didn't matter. I had my mind and that was all I needed. I began to apply myself in school. I quickly learned that all the negative things my father had told me about myself were not true. I realized that the anger he felt for the world didn't have to be mine. I also realized that the world could be a kind place, and that most people would do anything they could to help others, if they were just asked.

I dreamed of getting out of that little town. I dreamed of creating a successful life, so I began to apply myself in school. I realized that getting an education was the way I would find my personal freedom.

Then, like Keller, a teacher began to take an interest in me. She became my first mentor. As I went through my years in school, I made sure to find other teachers who could become my mentors. These mentors helped me create the life I had dreamed of as a young child. I would like to share the lessons that I learned from my mentors with you.If you apply these ideas to your life, nothing can stop you. You can do anything. There is no challenge you can't overcome.

YOUNG MAN, YOU ARE POWERFUL. YOU ARE MEANT FOR GREATNESS.

You will be knocked down in life. You will face adversity. You will lose. You will fail.

- But you will stand back up. You will finish the race.

People will treat you unfairly. People will judge you. Life will deal you terrible hands.

- But you are not a victim. You own your power.

You will meet those who loathe unity. You will encounter those who spread hate and create division.

- But you will help your people reach their potential.

When you perform at higher levels, you will face pressure. You will be tested by intensity.

- But you'll embrace the privilege of pressure. You've earned it! If the situation is brought to you, that should be a sign that you have the strength to handle it, or you will develop the strength. And that is a privilege — the opportunity to get stronger!

You will be sucker-punched. You will be beaten. You will be knocked down. Again. And again. And again. But you will keep fighting. You'll keep moving forward because you are a champion.

At some point you will realize that life isn't about you at all. This gift of living is so much bigger than all of us. This existence is an extraordinary opportunity to help people grow and reach their potential.

This day, this life, is your opportunity to make a difference. This is your chance. Stand up and take it.

SCARS ARE THE MEDALS OF CHAMPIONS

Your scars tell the story of a survivor.

Whether they are mental or physical, your scars are a testimony to your strength. They say to the world, "Knock me down. I will stand up stronger. Knock me down again. I will (still) continue to rise."

Your scars let the world know that there is a champion in the ring.

There is a warrior on the front line.

Be proud of your scars. Don't give up on life. Don't give up on yourself. You are a champion.

GET YOUR MIND RIGHT

Your mindset determines what happens in and around your life. The people you surround yourself with determine the same. They are a product of your mindset. And you are a product of their influence.

Are you growing? Or are you fixed? People with a growth mindset find valuable lessons in every failure. As a matter of fact, folks who have a growth mindset don't experience failure at all. When something goes wrong for them, they look at it as an opportunity to learn. They see the challenges in life as a way to grow.

People with a fixed mindset spend most of their time working to prove how smart or how talented they are by doing the most comfortable things they know. A person with a fixed mindset sees failure as a judgment of their character. The way they see it is, "If I fail at something, then I am a failure."

Live in the growth mindset. Look at every experience you encounter as a chance to grow and learn. You are not a failure. You will never be a failure. You are the type of person who is always learning, always getting better. You are always growing.

You are stronger than you know. You are more capable than you realize. You may even be greater than you can imagine.

SHOW UP TO THE GAME OF LIFE

What is one thing you can do to better yourself that requires no talent? Show up. A major mistake that many people make is believing that if they can't win, then there's no reason to try.

Losing is the very reason we try. Loss teaches us the most important lessons.

Never be afraid of losing. Never be afraid to show up. It takes massive courage to put one foot in front of the other and move forward. Be brave. Start stepping. Keep showing up day in and day out. Keep showing up when everybody else stays home. You will reach heights you never thought possible.

CHANGE YOUR THOUGHTS. CHANGE YOUR LIFE.

Your quality of life is determined by how you feel at any given moment.

Think about that. Think about turning this idea into a habit that would consistently promote positive, growth-oriented thoughts. What could that do for you?

What if you replaced your negative and doubtful thoughts with their opposites, with positive, empowering thoughts?

Give this a try. Every time you have a negative or doubtful thought, replace it with the opposite.

"I'm not smart enough..." becomes "I am smart enough..."

Try it for a single day. You may find some very interesting results.

BE THE TYPE OF PERSON WHO RESEMBLES A CHAMPION

Focus on becoming the person you dream to be. Your habits will move you towards becoming that type of person.

You can literally choose your identity by developing the habits that will transform you. You'll be amazed!

I am going to suggest to you the first 10 habits you should adopt, in order to begin your journey as a champion. These 10 habits can be worked on in the first 10 minutes of every day. That means you'll have 10 victories under your belt before most people have even woken up! I call this "10 Wins In 10 Minutes." If you do this, you will start every single day with a winning mindset.

1. Set a bedtime and go to bed on time.
2. Create a time to wake up and wake up on time. (Do not hit snooze.)
3. Sit with your eyes closed for 1-2 minutes and take deep breaths before getting out of bed.
4. Make your bed.
5. Drink 20-32 oz of water at room temperature.
6. Do some quick, light exercises or stretches.
7. Wash your face with cold water.
8. Brush your teeth.
9. Say a self-affirming statement five times in the mirror.
10. Play an uplifting theme song for the day.

Think about your day in this way, "I am becoming my habits. I am my habits." You don't rise to the level of your goals. You fall to the level of your habits. Success is not about goals. It's about habits and outcomes. Fall in love with the 'process,' not the 'goal.' Fall in love with the journey you are on.

People often reach goals and then revert to their old habits. People go through life, thinking, "Once I reach this goal, then I'll be happy." That's a very narrow version of happiness. Create a "systems first" mentality. You'll be happy anytime your system is running!

There was a great Kung Fu master named Bruce Lee. He is recognized as one of the most talented martial artists that ever lived. Here is his philosophy. Take it. Use it. Become the type of person who is a champion.

1. Research your own experience.

2. Absorb what is useful.
3. Reject what is useless.
4. Add what is specifically your own.

Time is irrelevant. The speed at which you finish things is irrelevant. The goal is irrelevant. It is the action that matters. Every moment is an experiment. Every experiment gives you a lesson.

Do something with the lessons your experiments give you. Apply those lessons to how you operate life. Be willing to fail and learn how to make sense of it. Every day offers fresh opportunities to find a better decision-making framework.

GET YOUR HABITS RIGHT. WIN THE GAME OF LIFE.

Anything is possible if you get your habits right. And it all starts with that first, tiny habit. It's referred to as a "keystone habit."

People try to change entire routines, diet, exercise. They start reading, meditating, and running. They quit things cold turkey, on and on... all at once. Then they get burned out. They get overwhelmed, injured, or they find that maintaining this new lifestyle is just too much of a hassle.

CHANGE JUST ONE HABIT.

You get up at the same time every day. You run down your street. You do 5-10 push-ups. That's it. One habit. Don't worry about anything else. That one habit becomes a "keystone habit," and it will snowball into other tiny habits, tiny wins that will add up quickly.

KEEP YOUR DREAMS ALIVE

As kids, we all had dreams of things we wanted to accomplish, but for many of us those dreams get shoved aside, and other things become a priority.

Not everyone has people in their life encouraging them to set high goals.Our family members pleaded with us to settle for average. Our teachers told us that we weren't smart enough or talented enough or strong enough.

We were constantly given reasons why we should put our dreams to rest and settle for what life gave us. After spending half of my life searching to find the dreams that I had as a boy, I am here to tell you- don't ever give up on your dreams. Your dreams may seem like they are a million miles away right now. You may hear people all around you saying, "Quit dreaming and get real. You can't do that."

Always remember this. When a person tells you that you "can't" do something, they are only saying that "they" can't do it.

Give yourself freedom to believe in your dreams. Never stop believing in your dreams.

Your dreams are the only reality. Remember, you can do anything.

YOUNG, GIFTED, AND...

By Shawn Mason

I'm fortunate. Fortunate, whether I truly listened to the words or not. Fortunate, even if they sounded like the mumblings of the teacher in every Charlie Brown TV special I watched as a little boy. Fortunate, because if I wanted to be disobedient to the message, I had to make the effort to tune it out. I had to purposely ignore it.

I had a loving father, a present big brother, and uncles-not to mention the wealth of women in my life. Sometimes questions were discreetly sprinkled into the conversations we would have about my future. What would I do?Who would I be? What would I be?

Those messages started on the day I was born. They continued to occur, even though my ability to understand them had not been realized. Even the "someday" conversations about all the great and amazing things I would experience and accomplish as a man were spoken of. Even the failures and losses that awaited. The victories. The defeats. The first kisses and the broken hearts. And the finding of love and the losing love conversations were all wildly accurate.

What I have come to realize is that, as a little boy, and at times even as a teen, I listened almost as if I was someone else, and that they would be doing the work. I listened as if, one day, I would simply wake up, look in the mirror, and be the man my collective villages had talked to me about. I guess, in a sense, that's how it happens. I'm sure that, as men, we all felt that moment in time when we looked in the mirror and, right or wrong, we actually saw a man in our reflection.

I was rarely mindful of the impact my experiences would inevitably have on the man I was going to be. I never really thought about the good or bad, being present once I had become a man. I was never one who had a problem with authority when it was executed fairly and without bias.

By the time I was a teen, I realized authority could be carried out with a malice I had no responsibility for, but it didn't blur my vision regarding the concept, and the place authority, had in my life.

At this point in my life, I know that young boys who can't handle or respect authority often grow up to be men with the same issue. They might even somehow look to glorify it in that toxic masculine way we often use to justify our counterproductive behavior.

Then, by the time I was a young adult, I realized that young boys who bully other boys and even girls, are likely the ones who exercise any authority they might have with the same malice I mentioned before. They likely handle women in the way that has eventually led to some of the much-needed movements we are so boldly advocating for today.

As a man, I realized that the earlier the failure to see or be shown the value of a woman in your life, means the likelihood of you never truly seeing it—ever. I don't mean only the romantic value associated with relationships and marriage, but the value that a woman has as a friend and a confidante. As a person. It's a failure that leads to the objectification of women at the highest level, and men who don't even understand their inability to see women as people: just... "things."

What little boy can ever truly fathom the weight of the things that life will show him over time? Not only about himself, but about the variety of men that will exist in the world around him that he may be unfairly associated with.

As a seasoned adult, I live in the value of those moments I had growing up daily. From the "someday" conversations I actually understood, to the ones so early in life that they would simply serve as seeds to be watered by the experiences ahead. The reality for me is that my life didn't become what I, or many in my village, foresaw. I concede that it has yet to become what I had hoped for. I was the one with the "gifts."

Honestly, I have felt cursed with them many times. Actually, I still battle with feeling cursed. Gifts create as many expectations from others as they do of the person who is the gifted one. Talent does not always yield fame or even success. Too many gifts can make you feel divided. Maybe it was just that way for me. I always felt divided. Like I had to commit to one to be great. The marriage of gift and passion never seemed consistent for me. If I was considered good at it, I didn't always have the hunger for it. If I was hungry for it, there were far too many people better at that thing than I felt I was. Sometimes I thought I simply feared greatness.

Yet, it was the collective conversations, experiences, and lessons that eventually gave me peace. Maybe even some of the things whispered in my ear as a baby. Eventually, I stumbled upon a brand-new gift and, over time, a brand-new understanding of what having a gift means.

At the time of this writing, I have found the courage to pursue my dreams and work, to live out this gift. Am I turning my back on the other gifts? Never. They have been tweaked and massaged at every age and every stage, and that will continue. I will never toss them away, even if I have finally found some peace in a particular one. However, I earnestly believe it took every single experience, lesson, victory, hurt, failure, broken heart, monumental moment, etc. to get to this place. I never had the courage to choose one of the gifts myself, so the Divine had the gift choose me.

So, what am I really trying to offer? Every chance I get to speak to a young person, and young boys, in particular, I tell them that what they do, even now, matters in determining the man they will become.

Don't sacrifice your childhood and all that it should be and mean for you. Don't carry the weight of the world on your shoulders before you have to. If life dictates you being adult-like sooner than you had hoped, then give your best, but if it doesn't, don't rush it. Live your life at each stage, but be aware that the things you do, learn, value, and represent during those years will leave their mark on you in manhood.

The man that finally sees himself in the mirror is just a product of the journeys taken by the little boy who is too new to the world to understand the someday predictions whispered in his ear. I know very few men that I knew as boys that are much different in manhood.

So, for every boy trying now to be a man... don't. Instead, be a boy who knows that he is on a journey to manhood, and that every day he is picking up something he could potentially take with him. And, for any man willing to mentor or share his personal experiences with boys, please give him something of substance that he can use so that, when he gets older, the man he becomes looks back at (him in) his reflection and be proud. I may not have realized every dream I had, or that others had for me, but I am pleased with the man I have become.

RUN YOUR RACE
By Eric Hampton

RACE

I must admit, I'm in a race. Most of us are in a race. To be more specific, most men or males are in a race. And it's ok to be in a race because most races have finish lines, but not all races have finish lines.

I'm not sure where I first heard of a "rat race," but I know I'll never forget its meaning or its implications. Rat races have starting points, but not finish lines. Rat races are never-ending and never fulfilling. Rat races are endless, and perhaps pointless.

Somehow, rats racing around an obstacle course for cheese can be compared to the human experience, and how we run around this world for temporary satisfaction.

We expend a large amount of energy to achieve something, but later find out it wasn't worth all that energy. Or perhaps we invest a lot of resources to obtain something, and later we find ourselves regretting using our resources in such a wasteful manner.

I, too, am guilty of using my means for meaningless things, because I found myself in a meaningless race.

Serving as the lead pastor in a church can certainly be a race. Some people measure pastors by the "3 B's": budget, building, and butts in seats. I never heard of such a thing, but somehow, I became hurled into this religious rat race. I began to worry excessively about our budget, especially because it continued to increase annually.

I began to worry about the building, and that we needed to be bigger and better to look successful, I began to worry that we would need more people to fill those seats, more services, and more, more, more… until I realized that I was running in someone else's race-not mine!

And one day, you may find yourself feeling discouraged and disgruntled because you are running in someone else's race. When you run your own race, no one is keeping time or keeping score. Your goal must be to move forward and finish strong. It is imperative that you are surrounded by people who care about you-not just the race you're running. They'll care for you when you're tired and inspire you to keep going when you want to quit.

Don't compare yourself to other marathon runners. Their race is none of your business, and your race is none of their business. Run your race and do what only you can do. And leave the results up to God!

REWARD

When my brother and I were little boys, we were taught to work hard and work smart. Our parents, our athletic heroes, and our spiritual leaders all mirrored and modeled this discipline. Many people believe that the discipline of work, of having a work ethic and ingenuity, does produce the results we all want and desire-but it may also produce unwanted and unhealthy results.

At some point, I became a self-diagnosed workaholic. I wasn't just studying, or preparing, or strategizing my craft, because I was taking it to another level. I wasn't sleeping because of work. My eating habits were horrible because of work. I was compulsively working long hours at the expense of my family. I was also sabotaging my own physical, spiritual, and emotional health. This went on for years and years because I never consistently applied the principle of rewarding myself.

Now I intentionally try to reward myself because I understand that it is essential to celebrate my hard work. Like me, you must also give yourself a pat on the back from time to time. When you achieve your short-term or long-term goals, you must also say to yourself, "Job well done!"

When we reward ourselves, our brain brilliantly releases a chemical called dopamine. This chemical is critical in magically making us feel good, regarding reward-motivated behaviors. This inner feeling energizes us and pushes us forward to achieve our next set of goals.

In school, the teacher may give you a sticker as a reward, but as you mature, perhaps your reward is enjoying chicken wings with friends, or planning a fun outing, like a vacation, with your family. So, life is short. You are an amazing, hard-working person. Your results deserve a reward, big or small. Celebrate each and every accomplishment. Don't take anything for granted. Like me, you will find that even a small reward will serve as a great motivator to keep you going further, faster!

LEARN TO PLAY TO JAZZ
By Kenery Kent Smith

As a Black Man in America, you are constantly navigating your way through the forces from without that will seek to limit you, and the forces from within that will seek to define you, knowing that your mental, spiritual, and emotional latitude and longitude, at all times, is tantamount to truly knowing who you are. Other men will try to quantify you. Women will seek to qualify you.

You will be held up, measured, inspected, counted, analyzed, sorted, dismissed, recalled, scrutinized, excluded, blamed, rejected, falsely accused, unfairly uncredited, unrecompensed, stolen from, misinterpreted, misinformed, and mischaracterized. The world will stand you in the town square, put you on display like property, check your teeth, and look up the crack of your behind.

It will clutch its collective purse, cross its existential street to avoid walking on the same side as you, and it will constantly tell you that it doesn't see color—that everything isn't about "race." All of this will be done by measuring sticks being held up against you for things that you either have no control over, such as your melanin count, or the socioeconomic status you were born into. Or there will be characterizations based on antiquated, unrealistic, and frankly non-Black value systems that have been foolishly, blindly adapted into a culture that is constantly being kept from standing on equal footing with the culture from whence said values were derived.

There will be "lists" presented to deem your worthiness of a woman's respect, let alone her loyalty or love. There will be numbers you'll need to add up to, and statuses you'll be required to live up to, simply to qualify for her love. And this will all be done in an attempt to put you into a nice, neat little check box on a list of "desirable attributes" to be brought to a fictional "table." Or it will be on an application for a school or a job, or when you buy your first car. Rent your first apartment. Buy your first home. Move into your first nice neighborhood. However, you will learn that, in spite of it all, as a Black Man in 'Murica, you can learn to navigate it all. You can find your way through the miasma, through the macro and micro aggressions, through the rejections, the disappointments, and the heartbreaks.

To be, in the wise words of Bruce Lee, "like water." To improvise. If you learn how to play Jazz. Like a beautifully flowing improvised melody, the space you occupy today won't be quite the same as the one you will inhabit tomorrow. Yes, there will be times when you will hit some bad notes; in this way, life is more akin to Jazz Music than it is to Classical. Classical Music, while it has its version of passionate expression, is very structured, with no improvisation of the notes as written allowed. Jazz, on the other hand... well, the whole beauty of Jazz is in its ability to evolve. A Classic Jazz song will never be played quite the same way twice—even by the same person.

Jazz lives... and it breathes. As with life, Jazz is never stagnant unless you allow it to be, because living a beautiful life is about so much more than just hitting the right notes as written. It's about phrasing. It's about intent and purpose. It's about taking chances with the notes of our existence that may or may not seem to fit together from a logical, theoretical point of view.

Instead, life is about weaving together a series of notes... a string of events... in order to tell a story. A great and wonderful story, one which has meaning to the teller, as well as to anyone who hears/sees/reads it. Living a beautiful life is akin to managing structured chaos. It would be equivalent to that beautiful Jazz melody you would create on your instrument of choice, in order to express to the world who your innermost you is. Except that, every now and then, the band leader will abruptly change the key of the song. Or the tempo. Or the actual musical genre. Or the venue you're playing in. Or the instrument you are playing on. And sometimes, while you are playing your melody, even the band members will change; old familiar ones will leave, and new unknown ones will suddenly appear. They will come and go as the music dictates. But, as the lyrics to a famous Jazz standard states, the melody... your melody... still lingers on.

You may be forced to adjust your notes here and there, because you, of course, want, above all else, the music to sound great. For your life to BE great. But there will be sour notes. It is almost inevitable. However, whether or not those bad notes will actually ruin the song is totally dependent upon how you respond to them.

The great Miles Davis famously said, "There's no such thing as a wrong note... It's not the note you play that's the wrong note—it's the note you play afterwards that makes it right or wrong." And that, my friend, is also life. When you make mistakes... when unplanned and unwanted things happen to you and AT you, you likely won't have any control over

when they occur. But what you will always have control of... is the note you play afterwards. Learn to play your life as well as Coltrane played his saxophone. Embrace your life-bad notes and all. You still can make beautiful music, even when the tune seems to be going sour. But when you know who you are... WHOSE you are... then you'll find that the well that you can tap into within yourself and without in the universe, is full of unmatched potential, and unlimited note choices.

Hey, Black man. Young Brother. Wide-eyed little boy in the ghetto. I implore and advise you: Learn the art of improvisation in your life. Learn about what is deep inside of you,

waiting to be birthed and manifested. Learn to play that beautiful note that can come right after the bad one hits. Learn to play Jazz.

THE LIFE-LONG JOURNEY
By Lionel Hilaire

Cause I Look Haitian

Lionel, nice to meet you. First bump.
Little does he know, I'm a ticking time bomb.

Sixth grade is when my life took a shift.
Back to school, Dad gave Momma $100 for 4 kids.

How can I make this work? Mommy in her thoughts.
Like many Haitians, we went to the Swap Shop.

First day of school, I swore I'm fresh.
Shirt, pants, and shoes all on deck.

Walking on campus, happy as I can be.
Knew I was the funk 'cause all eyes are on me.

For the first time in my life, I was winning.
'Cause primary school was a rough beginning.
But no looking back, I love the new me.
My future was bright as far as I could see.

First period was great, onto the next class.
I'm so clean, no need to walk fast.

I'm proud of myself, head held high.
I'm liking school, for the very first time.

Then BANG! Is all I hear.
My head hits the wall, ringing in my ear.

I thought somehow, this was a mistake.
Someone will apologize and I'll be on my way.

As I turn around, I see 30 boys.
I'm trying to calm down, but my head is hearing noise.

Now I'm ready to fight, my emotions changed.
I came to school happy and now I'm enraged.

These boys told me I'm not one of them and I was faking.
I don't fit in 'cause I look Haitian.
All this time, I thought we were one.
Now I see the difference and that's no fun.

Thinking it was over, I went back to school.
It happened again; guess I am the fool.

From then on, they never saw my face.
Bus dropped us off, I hit the gates.

I'm grateful I can read and write today.
I barely attended school, I credit God's Grace.

Today giving back is what I do best.
I forgave those boys, now they're off my chest.

I wrote a book for them, but some are dead or in prison.
I challenge other men to join me on this mission.
Let's help men heal the boy within.
Because if they're restored, we all win!

I remember my father sharing his story with me about his near-death experience and struggle in Haiti. With passion in his eyes and voice, Dad mentioned how corrupt and dangerous the Haitian government was under the evil dictatorship of Jean-Claude "Baby Doc" Duvalier. Haitians were constantly beat and murdered if they went against their President's laws and commands, he said.

My dad went on to share how many Haitians began to flee the country. "I would help many of the people get on boats and sail to Miami," Dad said. Haitians called the United States "Miami." Later, he was captured while he was helping the people escape Haiti. "I was arrested and beaten for about 14 days because of it. Beaten until I was unrecognizable!" I was shocked as I listened to him share his story with me when I was a young boy. Somehow my dad was released from custody.

In the late 70's, and through to the early 80's, hundreds of thousands of Haitians continued to flee the small Island of Haiti. These people were often referred to as refugees. Black Americans who were born here, made fun of, and teased them, saying Haitians came to America on "The Banana Boat." My mom and dad were among those who escaped. When they arrived in America, my dad worked many jobs, but spent most of his years working in construction and building many homes in the cities of Coral Springs and Weston, Florida. (My mom was home for several years until she began working as a janitor at Florida Atlantic University.)

My father faced a near-death experience, escaped from a cruel country on a 7-day boat ride with very limited food and water. Once he arrived in America, he worked very hard. From what I learned, society said a man needs to protect and provide for his family. When it came to protection, my father was in the home. Dad couldn't read or write, but he bought us our first home in 1985. Him being there and having a roof over our heads allowed me to feel protected and safe. Protection wasn't a challenge for him.

When it came to providing, our lights and water were never turned off. We always had food in the refrigerator. I never heard my parents argue over bills. If there was a "societal checklist," for my dad, it would look like this:

- Protect Your Family
- Provide for Your Family

But there was one "P" society missed. This "P" can be known as the all-time thing men and boys like myself craved but missed. The third piece that should be added to the "societal checklist" is called "Present." I like to say it like this: my dad was in the home, but he wasn't of the home. He lived in the home, but he wasn't involved with the affairs of the home.

Looking back now, I needed my dad to:

- Sit with me and show me how to tie my shoelaces.
- Have that talk about girls and how to treat them.
- Teach me the importance of sex.
- Show me how to drive a car.
- What to do if I get pulled over by the police.
- Teach me how to go from a boy to a man.
- Affirm me as a man.
- Show me how to be an effective husband and father.
- Say, "I love you no matter what, son."
- Joke, laugh, dance, and play with me.
- Take me out just because.

This is what being of the home would look like to me when I needed it the most. Instead, for my dad, the "societal checklist" looked like this:

- Protect Your Family
- Provide for Your Family
- Be Present in Your Family

"Being present" was the one area my dad would not receive a check mark for on the "societal check list". This doesn't make my dad a bad person. He did the best he knew how to do, and I respect that. However, this does not take away from the fact that his best, or any father's best, can cause years of heartache, pain, and resentment to their children.

Being present is key to raising children to become healthy, positive, and effective adults.

It was time for sixth grade. I can remember it like it was yesterday. My mom went to my dad and asked him for back-to-school money for myself, my sister, and my two brothers so we could buy clothes and supplies. Dad handed my mom $100 for four kids! $100 can barely buy a week's worth of clothes for one child—even in the mid 90's! My dad stood firm and didn't budge to give more, even after we all fussed and argued about him giving us more money.

My mom did what many Haitians who had limited funds did by taking the four of us shopping at the Swap Shop. The Swap Shop is where you go to find bargains and, in the 90's, fake designer clothing. It's like going to the biggest yard sale in the world. Until this day, I don't know how my mom managed to successfully purchase clothes for four children to go back to school, but this determined lady made it happen. Thanks, Mom!

Now it's the first day of 6th grade and I am excited. Looking at my outfit and the thoughts of having a fresh start had me smiling from ear to ear. I can remember feeling so thrilled to start middle school. It felt so great to become a big boy now. Another first for me was riding a school bus and having my own clothes—not the ones passed down from my older brother James.

Yes! The bus ride to school was great. Breakfast was delicious and now it's time for class. After my first period, I was walking the hallways loving my new clothes and new shoes. Then, all of a sudden... BANG!!! My head hits the wall and I'm thinking this is some type of mistake. Someone will apologize and I'll be on my way. I turn around and see about 30 boys. Looked like they made the smallest one hit me. Now

I'm angry and afraid at the same time. I put up my fists to fight 'cause I know I can't show any sign of fear. My friend Willie pulled me back and walked me to class.

Later I found out that the reason I was punched was because I looked Haitian. I went to school the next day and it happened again. These bullies went as far as to make every Friday "Haitian Day," a day where they would find boys who looked Haitian and punch them in the face. And, because of this, many of us boys left the school campus right after the school bus dropped us off. Oftentimes, we would hop on the city bus and head to Fort Lauderdale beach. For just about the entire year of 6th grade, Fort Lauderdale beach is where you would find me.

FATHER FIGURE
By Mel Roberson

The first snowfall of the year had just taken place in Chicago. A man in his early 70's sits at his kitchen table looking out of his back window at the light white dusting covering his pick-up truck. He smiles as he sits there thinking about the beauty of life. The smell of smothered potatoes fills the air because he has started the breakfast making process. His oldest son enters the kitchen, about 37 years of age, to check on his father.You can tell that there was a bond there... a closeness that not all men get to experience with their fathers.This had not always been the case with their relationship though.

The reason that they were so close was because his father had almost died the previous year. There was a certain sense of urgency about spending time with family now, something that made the son almost forget all the times his father had made him mad or let him down. There was also a certain amount of fear that the son had every time he looked at his father. He wasn't afraid of his father... he was afraid of losing him.That son was me.

On that morning I had a conversation with my father that was a little different from any other one we had ever had. Don't get me wrong, we had a good relationship. My dad was... is... my hero. I have learned a lot about being a man from him.Yet, no man is perfect. We have talked about the times where I felt he dropped the ball, and the times where I have dropped the ball. All relationships are two-way streets. Children have responsibilities too, and parents should do their best to guide them through various stages of life. Now, back to the conversation.

That year showed me how fragile life is, and how valuable time is, for the second time in my life. The first time was when I was 17 years old. I was shot in an attempted carjacking in Chicago. I lived to tell the story, obviously. Anyway, my dad almost losing his life shook me to my core. I didn't and still don't know what life would be like without him physically here. The conversation that morning though... It gave me a new perspective on life and learning from my family.

I have always been a learner, so to speak. I hold several degrees, and I have a library in my home office that rivals that of a small private school, with books on several different topics. Up to the point of that very pivotal conversation though, I had never been a learner of life from a conversational perspective. Like... My dad taught me how to drive, change oil on a car, how to change a tire, and other things throughout my life, but he never had a conversation with me just about life itself.

I could go into specific details about my conversation with him, but that is not the main point of this story. I want to pull out one specific phrase that he said that day that I had probably heard before, but I heard it in a totally different way that morning.

We were talking about times in his life when he wished that he had listened to what other people were telling him, people that were trusted resources and had his best interests in mind, and he said, "If I knew then what I know now..." Of course, I had heard people use that phrase before. I even used it myself. That morning though, it hit me differently. I am not sure why, but I heard him differently. It landed differently. I processed it differently and acted on his words differently.

Since then, I have had so many conversations with my father that I will never forget. However, this was just an extremely long set up to get to what I really need to tell you. "If I knew then what I know now" is a thief of experience. If you really had access to the information in those cases, there may have been valuable lessons that you lost because of what you had to learn. I am not saying that you should do everything on your own without heeding the advice of trusted counsel. What I am saying is that the Universe knows when to allow you to bump your head and learn a lesson the hard way. There needs to be a mixture of lessons and experiences that help to shape a man. Yes, there are some things that I wish I would have known ahead of time.In many of those cases though, I would not be the man I am today without the tough lessons that only experience could have taught me.

My children were 11 and 21 at the time that my father fell ill.I have two amazing daughters. They literally are my reasons for existing.I would walk to the ends of the earth for them because I love them beyond measure.I often reflect on my younger years wondering what I would have changed so that I could have been a better person. I don't know I can say that there is much that I would have changed.I am a comic book nerd, and I think that changing the smallest thing in the past may throw off the entire space and time continuum: Like...when superheroes travel back in time in comics, they are extremely careful not to make any changes—the slightest changes in an event could alter history.

I'm grateful for all my experiences because of what I've learned from them.If I would have stayed away from an argument that I had with my college girlfriend, would I still be the father that I am today? Would my children even exist as I know them? Would I have the life that I have grown to love? The real answer is I do not know. Some people say that they don't regret anything.I am not one of those people. I have a ton of regrets from mistakes that I made, people I mistreated, and situations that left me heartbroken. However, I took those experiences that could be perceived as negative and extracted lessons from them. Those are the things that have made me the man that I am today.I honestly believe that the hardships I experienced made me a better man, and a better father.

Here is what I would say, though.It is easy for me to say in reflection what I think I would have changed, or what I wish I would have done differently. What I would really want you to take away from this is that you should make the best decision with the information you have at the time. There will be times that you have good information, and you still make bad decisions. Those moments are when you have to live with the consequences of your actions. The best way to get better answers in life is to ask better questions. I've learned to live with the decisions I have made. However, I wish I would have had the following list of questions earlier in life, to help me make my decision process more efficient:

1. Am I making the best decision with the information that I have at this time? (I gave you this one already)
2. Do I have enough information right now?
3. THIS IS A HUGE ONE! Do I stand to lose more than I stand to gain?
4. How will this decision impact the people involved?
5. Am I prepared to live with the potential consequences of my actions?

Those are the things that I ask myself in a lot of situations. I could try to give you advice all day long based on my personal experiences. Again, you will have to learn some things on your own. There is absolutely nothing wrong with getting good advice from people that you trust. Even in those situations you can still ask yourself those questions.When you have to make decisions on your own, you can still ask those questions.

I'm sorry if this hasn't been groundbreaking or earth-shattering for you. I have discovered that some of the most valuable lessons have come in the simplest forms. I have also discovered that there is no cookie cutter answer to everything. People need to walk their own paths and figure out what works for them.I initially was going to take you on a journey through my experiences as a father, but this is what showed up when my fingers started hitting the keyboard. My prayer is that it lands with the person that needs to hear this at the right time, sothey can begin to make the best decisions with the information they have at the time.

FAMILY MATTERS
By Robert Hazzard, Jr.

To my grandboys, Lyric, Noah, and BJ. Let me share a story of growing up on the southside of Chicago, right outside of the Chatham area. It was back in the 1970s when the family was everything, and the most important and central focal point.

I was the only boy in a family of three girls, so just imagine what that was like living in a house and having no boys to play with as I was growing up. The super cool thing was that, by being the only boy, it afforded my dad the opportunity to shower me with G.I. Joe's or Superman action figures to play with. Life back then was fun and exciting for several reasons.

My mom and dad worked hard to ensure that we knew what the basic family foundational structure should look like. For example, love and respect was something we observed daily that was demonstrated in our house between our parents.

As a kid growing up, it was normal to speak to our neighbors on the block, and even hang out in their homes, because it was not as difficult to trust them the way it is today. I remember being a crossing guard during my time in grammar school when I began to like girls, and it helped that I wore an orange safety belt after school. As a junior safety person, I helped ensure people made it across the street safely.

It was also during this time period that we had policemen visit our school on a regular basis, telling us that we can trust them to protect us. I think the program was called "D.A.R.E.," and a police officer was referred to as, "Officer Friendly." I mentioned earlier that my family taught us to show respect to others, especially leaders or authority figures like teachers and police officers? Well, that became ingrained in my head as I got older.

Remember those action figures I played with from back in the day, G.I. Joe and Superman? I wanted to be Superman to the young girls and save Lois Lane from harm, or at least from the other boys. LOL, as I got older, I wanted to be that officer friendly guy so much that I joined a program the Chicago Police Department came up with called, "The Police Explorers." So, from age 14 to 16, I went to local police meetings, and even had an ID card and wore a blue uniform. Talk about fun! I quickly learned that girls back then liked a guy in uniform, but that immediately changed once I experienced racism from white police officers. It didn't matter how many meetings I attended, or that I was perceived as a good kid from a nice neighborhood and had both parents in our household. Certain police saw me as a black kid and targeted me just like they did other black kids.

FATHER INVOLVEMENT

Being the only boy out of four kids had some advantages, when you think about it. I did not have to share my new bike or boy stuff with my sisters or worry about hand me down clothes. I got to be spoiled, which years later included a cool white Chevy Camaro, although that had to be shared with my older sister. I asked my dad how do you share a car? It was a teachable moment for sure.

There was a lot of teaching and lesson learning growing up in the Hazzard household. Now for sports. My parents wanted me involved in baseball, bowling, basketball, and track, and it was later that I learned why. It was not for the reasons I thought, but it was for father and son moments that included coaching from the side lines.

All these activities related back to the idea of sharing. Share the spotlight, be a team player, respect others, and learn to stay in my lane, much like I had to do with my sisters when I was growing up.

I happened to be a fairly good bowler back in the day, so every Saturday morning that's where you could find me and my dad. As the team captain, I was expected to help us win the game and a big trophy at the end of the season. Unlike some of the other boys on the block, I got taught how to fix things around the house and work on machines, since my dad was a mechanic. Those teachings would come in handy later in life once I bought my own home.

RELATIONSHIP TRAINING

You would think that growing up with sisters I might have picked up a few tips and tricks on how to date. Nope! Like most young boys, we got our advice from the guys at the barbershop, which did not really work. Some of the advice was so far-fetched now that, thinking back on it, that was probably why it never worked, or why relationships didn't last that long. So, what is a boy to do? Turn to your mom for advice when all else fails and her famous words, "I can't teach you how to be a man, but your dad can." While my dad might have been a lady's man prior to getting married, I was not so sure his wisdom would work today, and his suggestions always directed me back to reading my bible and connecting with singles in church. So, after a few failed marriages, it became clear that the lesson about understanding love required a do-over class.

So, let me leave you with this. Real relationships matter and are built on respect, trust, integrity, character and, most importantly, love.

THE LESSONS CONTINUE
By Carlo Kennedy

WHAT I'VE LEARNED...

I'm one of those people you read about after they're dead. One of those authors who wrote books that helped or inspired people, but then you find out their personal life was messed up.

 In spite of all my career success—tenured professor and author of a bunch of books, I've also seen a lot of failure in my life; including two wives that divorced me. I won't torture you with the details of my two failed marriages, but I will tell you this: I am still a romantic person, and I am still optimistic that marriage can be a source of true happiness, and that it IS God's will for most of us. In other words, in spite of my failures, I'm still hopeful. And after all the crap I went through, some of it was my own fault, but a lot of it wasn't-and now life is good. So, in this chapter, I'm going to tell you what I've learned through my experiences—through all the pain and suffering of my failures. And my hope is that what I've learned will help you avoid some of the mistakes I made. Don't get me wrong. You will make your own mistakes and, although my experiences can't prevent you from making mistakes altogether, at least maybe some of this stuff will help you recover from your own mistakes more quickly, and without being too hard on yourself for making them. So, here's what I've learned.

WHAT I'VE LEARNED ABOUT LIFE

A lot of people waste the present by trying too hard, or spending too much time, planning the future. I used to think that making the most out of life meant controlling the future, getting it all figured out, so the future would work out perfectly. But it doesn't work that way.

Sure, you have to figure out what makes you happy, and you do have to plan for the future in some ways—like saving money. But, beyond that, it's not about planning; it's more about learning to live with gratitude, contentment, and peace. That's because no one really knows what's best in their future, and even if you did know what would be best, you would not know how to make it happen. More often than not, by trying to make it better, you would make it worse. That's what happened to me.

I spent a lot of time and money over the years trying to promote myself as a musician, a public speaker, and an author, and most of it went nowhere. I spent a lot of time and energy trying to do things that people would now call building a "platform," or a "brand," and most of it was a big waste. Not only that, I know now that if I had achieved some of the big dreams I had, it would not have made me happy anyway.

People of faith talk about wanting to do God's will—and that's a good thing. But it turns out that doing God's will is not about figuring out God's will and then making that happen. It's about dealing with whatever God gives you today. Life is not about trying to force God's will into being in the future. Getting the most out of life is actually about living a simpler, less complicated life, by just doing what's right today, and not wasting today planning on tomorrow and taking time for gratitude.

I'm very grateful that I've been able to get my career to the point where I can live the lifestyle of a professor and author. But, even that, getting to where I am, has not been the result of me making good decisions, so much as just walking through the doors that have opened for me, and finally letting go of the doors that were closed to me. That expression about God opening a window when he closes a door has turned out to be wiser than I ever imagined, because it is only God who does the opening and closing; the doors that I have forced open have all turned out to be disasters. Other doors that I tried to push open were never going to open for me, so I wasted a lot of time and energy focusing on things that were not God's will for me. But, in spite of my failures, I actually have a great life now.

I have the perfect job for me, and a woman who appreciates me and treats me like a king—and I treat her like a queen. But none of this came about because I planned it. I am where I am in life because I stumbled through the doors that God opened for me. Everything good I have is a gift from God. I did not earn it, and I could not have made it happen, no matter how many good decisions I made.

So, I've learned that God's will for us is more about being than doing. Figuring out God's will for us is not about making pros and cons lists and laboring over big decisions. It's also not about what career path to take, or even who to marry. Doing God's will means being the man God wants you to be, no matter what job you find yourself in, or who you marry. There's a passage in the Bible, in the apostle Paul's letter to the Galatians, where he talks about what he calls the "Fruit of the Spirit;" that is, the produce, or product, of having the Holy Spirit within you, guiding you (Galatians 5:22-23). The fruits of the Spirit are love, joy, peace, patience, kindness, generosity, faithfulness, gentleness, and self-control. So, do you want to know what God's will for you is? God's will for you is to be a loving man, a joyful man, and a man of peace. His will is for you to be patient, kind, and generous-to be faithful, gentle, and to be a man of discipline. That's God's will for you. If you work on these things, the other stuff will fall into place.

WHAT I'VE LEARNED ABOUT SUCCESS

I've learned that success means not letting anyone else define success for you. Every man needs to define success for himself, and not just assume that his definition of success will match other peoples.' If you try to live up to another person's definition of success, and it's not right for you, it will only cause you anxiety, and you'll probably die too young. And if you're living with anxiety right now, that may be a sign that you are trying to live up to someone else's expectations about what success is.

Success is not measured in dollars or in square feet, but in time. A successful life is one that gives you enough free time to do what makes you happy, and what God has given you to do. So, for example, one man's successful life might mean becoming a surgeon, and healing people—but that would mean working long hours every week throughout the year; while another man's successful life might mean becoming a teacher so he can have summers off to do missionary work, or volunteer at a summer camp, or write inspirational books. Is the teacher less successful because he makes less money? Or because he lives in a smaller house or drives an older car? No!

That's because success has very little to do with money or possessions; it has everything to do with lifestyle. The man in the $100,000 car stuck in a traffic jam every day is much less happy than the man in the $5,000 car who works five minutes from his home. In fact, it's important to understand that success is not a state of being—you don't "arrive" at success, and then just sit back and enjoy it. Success is a lifestyle, and, no matter what you do, your life will change constantly over the years, and you will always be re-evaluating, and re-defining success for each new phase of your life. I can't say this strongly enough. Success is not arriving at a point; success is living a lifestyle. It means to live faithfully one day at a time, doing your best to be faithful in each moment, working on becoming the best person you can be, and using your free time to share the gifts God has given you with others. Success is not about getting somewhere. Success is being part of something bigger than yourself and becoming someone who is the best possible version of what God made you to be.

When I was young, I had this idea about me "making it" and leaving my mark on the world. For me that was a dream of being a rock star—or at least a famous songwriter. That never happened. I have become a successful author, but even when you write books, they can go out of print; they are not eternal. Nothing like that really lasts. Maybe you have dreamed about being a musician, or a music producer. Maybe you have dreamed of the power it would bring you if you could make a lot of money doing that. Or maybe you've dreamed about being a professional athlete, or some other career that would make you famous. And maybe you will accomplish that goal, but I know this much: leaving your mark on the world is not about having fans—it's about having a family.

If you want to leave this world with a legacy, the only thing that really lasts is to form a faithful household, raise faithful kids, and teach them how to make the world a better place. And if you don't end up having kids of your own, adopt some kids that need a good home. Build relationships with your relatives. Take care of your parents as they get older. Put down roots and become part of a community and get to know your neighbors!

WHAT I'VE LEARNED ABOUT PRIDE

We grow up being taught that when you accomplish good things, you should be proud of yourself. And my parents and grandparents were great—they were always telling me they were proud of me. And that was important for me because it gave me confidence. But the shadow side of that is that it made me assume I could rely on my own intelligence, strength, or even good looks to get ahead in life. And sometimes that worked. At other times, my pride got me in trouble-like when I didn't ask for help, just because I was too embarrassed to admit that I needed it. Everyone needs help. Ask for help when you can't handle everything all by yourself.

We often forget that pride is actually a sin. Everything I've learned about spirituality, especially the spirituality of the saints, friars, and monks, is that it's all about humility. That's the opposite of pride. And learning to trust in God and rely on him—that's the opposite of self-reliance. Pride is the reason people ignore God and assume they don't need God in their lives—and some even believe that God doesn't exist.

There's a lot of talk in some circles about being an "alpha male." This comes from research that people have done studying dogs and wolves. The leader of a pack of dogs or wolves is referred to as the alpha dog. That's because "alpha" is the first letter in the Greek alphabet. So, the first dog, or the "top dog," is the alpha dog. But people are not dogs—or at least they shouldn't be. And the whole "alpha male" concept usually just ends up with men and women being enemies. I prefer to think of it a different way.

There's a theory that says that there are three kinds of people: sheep, wolves, and sheepdogs. The sheep are most people, going about their business; innocent, but vulnerable, and these are the ones who are in danger of becoming the victims of the wolves. The wolves are the predators. The people who live like God isn't watching, as if anything is acceptable, as long as you can get away with it. These are the people who take advantage of weaker people—either through violence, manipulation, or exploitation. Wolves are everywhere. Every day you probably get emails from them trying to scam you. But the sheepdogs are the people who protect the sheep from the wolves.

People like police officers, military personnel, or other aware, prepared, and caring citizens. The sheep are often oblivious to danger until something bad happens. But the wolves are always out there, always looking for an opportunity to take something from you. The sheepdogs are the ones who are observant, vigilant, and who are ready to protect the sheep. The "alpha male" is really someone who is out for himself. Don't be an alpha male because, at the end of the day, the alpha is a wolf. The alpha takes pride to the extreme, to the point where he is a lone wolf—alone and bitter, angry with all the women who don't want to be with him because he's a wolf. Don't be a wolf. But don't be a sheep, either. Be a sheepdog. Learn to be aware of your surroundings. Be someone who cares about others and protects others from the wolves that are out there. And remember—the sheepdog works for the Shepherd.

WHAT I'VE LEARNED ABOUT LOVE

There's a song from the 90s by the group DC Talk. The song is called Love is a Verb. We usually think of love as an emotion, but when we think of it that way, we're really only thinking about one small part of romantic love. There is so much more to love than warm feelings. Real love is active. It's not what you feel, it's what you do. The feeling is the motivation for action, like when you go out of your way to do something nice for someone you love. But what happens when that feeling fades, or other things stress you out and overshadow the feelings of love? That's when the truth comes out. And the truth is, love is a choice. When you really love someone, it's not because you're both attracted to each other, it's not because you have some "chemistry," or you like to do the same things, or you have the same values—though all those things help. When you really love someone, it's because you've decided to love that person, and you've decided to love that person even if things change. Because things always change.

There is no perfect lover other than God, so, even in the best relationship, there will be times when the love energy is low—and that's when the decision to love carries the couple. In the Bible, the heart is not thought of as the place where emotions come from; it's thought of as the place where decisions come from. To love another person is to decide to love that person—not just as long as the feeling of attraction lasts, but as a commitment. It is a choice to love a person, to commit to serving that person, to vow to fight for that person. If both people do that, and, as long as both people do that, love will thrive, and it will increase.But this means that love can't be selfish. It has to be selfless, self-giving, a life of service—a labor of love.

I've learned that love has a lot to do with being loved. In other words, attraction goes a lot deeper than a person's looks. The way a person treats you is what really makes them attractive to you. If you choose a wife who treats you well, she will be attractive to you forever, no matter how her looks might change. If you choose a wife who makes you feel small, you will lose your attraction to her, no matter how hot she is. Marry someone who will treat you like a king and make you feel wanted and appreciated. That will make you want to love her in an action kind of way, and that will make her love you even more, and treat you right forever. The energy needed for loving comes from being loved. It's a snowball rolling downhill, getting bigger and bigger. Your love and service for her fuels her love and service for you, which, in turn, fuels your love and service for her.

But if you have to work too hard to gain the affections of a woman, she probably doesn't really want you. And life is too short to humiliate yourself for a woman who doesn't want you. The trick is to find the balance. Be humble enough to be willing to serve your woman, but don't demean yourself or compromise your values for a woman who won't serve you. Love yourself enough to marry a woman who will respect you, but don't be too proud to say you're sorry when you're wrong, or to go out of your way to show your love with actions.

WHAT I'VE LEARNED ABOUT GOD & PRAYER

God is not a vending machine. And prayer is not about asking for things for ourselves. When I was younger, I believed those people who said that you need to pray very specifically and tell God exactly what you want. But I've learned that that's wrong. That is telling God what to do, and that's not our place. This is especially true when it comes to praying for other people.

So many of my prayers were about asking God to make someone do something, or to prevent someone from doing something. The truth is, God will not take away anyone's free will. He will not make someone go to church, no matter how hard we pray for that, and he will not stop someone from drinking too much, or whatever their problem is—even though it's clear that that is his will. We actually need to pray LESS specifically because we just do not know what's best for us, or for the other people we pray for. I'm not saying that you can't ask for things in prayer; just do it with that humility I was talking about, the humility that admits you're not God, and you don't know what's best. Let God handle it. And when it comes to praying for yourself, spend more time asking God to change YOU, rather than asking him to change your circumstances.

WHAT I'VE LEARNED ABOUT SUFFERING

Suffering is a purifying fire, like the fire that purifies gold, and it purifies us by burning away the impurities of life and leaving us with what is essential and God-given. Don't get me wrong here. I'm not saying that God causes suffering because it's good for you. God does not cause suffering, and suffering is not good. Much suffering is of our own making. Other suffering comes from the world, or from an attachment to the things of the world. God doesn't cause the suffering, but he allows it to cleanse us. Suffering reminds us what is important in life, and it makes us more grateful for the gifts of God—even the little ones we often take for granted. Sometimes suffering forces us to get rid of the things that are holding us down. Also, suffering teaches us humility and compassion. If we can recognize our own responsibility for some of our own suffering, that should give us some compassion for others who are as flawed as we are. Suffering is a natural part of a fallen world, the natural result of sin. So, we should not be surprised by it. I'm not trying to explain it away; sometimes suffering is just tragic and there is no explanation for it.

A lot of my suffering has also come from me trying so hard to fix a future, and/or force things, that they never happened. I would respond to problems by trying all that much harder to control the outcome of the situation, and that only made it worse. A lot of anxiety is about not knowing the future, or the unknown of the long term. But trying to see and organize the long term often results in disaster. I've learned to let go of that need to organize the future and be at peace with the unknown. That's partly what it means to trust God. And if I can give myself credit for one mistake I didn't make—I didn't give up on God. I knew enough not to blame God for my suffering, and so, even though there were times when it was hard to talk to God, I never walked away from God. And God never walked away from me.

WHAT I'VE LEARNED ABOUT PEACE

I've learned that peace does not come from having everything you want. That's partly because there will always be more things to want-especially in our culture that is so obsessed with things. In reality, peace comes from letting go of having to get things, detaching yourself from "stuff," and simplifying your life. Another way to say this is that you don't get peace by getting what you want; you get peace by learning to appreciate what you already have.

Peace is the opposite of stress, and a man needs to detach from the things that cause him stress. One of the biggest things that cause stress in a man's life is drama. By that I mean getting involved in controversy, ongoing arguments, holding grudges, stuff like that. Peace comes from letting go of all of that, and especially from forgiving people who have wronged us. You know, Jesus said that refusing to forgive is one of the worst sins you can commit (see Matthew 6:14-15.) But we often sabotage our own peace with an assertive attitude, letting pride drive us to increase the drama, when it's really in our own best interest to get rid of it. In fact, I would say that attitude is one of the worst enemies of peace. This is part of the problem with the whole "alpha male" thing—too much attitude, too much pride.

Other enemies of a man's peace are multitasking, being over-scheduled, and spending too much time online. If we fill all our time with multi-sensory entertainment screens, it leaves no room for deep thought. It is peace and quiet that make room for God and the things of the Spirit in our lives. Turn off the device and read a book. Real men read books—especially the Bible. And the added benefit is that, when you read a book, it forces you to use your imagination, making you more creative.

If you feel like you need to chase after something, it will probably not bring you peace. If it takes effort to follow a trend, it will probably not bring you peace. If people make you feel bad for who you are or what you believe, then being around them will probably not bring you peace.

WHAT I'VE LEARNED ABOUT HAPPINESS

So, putting it all together, here are some things I hope you will remember.

First of all, learn the difference between drama and excitement, and between peace and boredom. Do not seek or create drama because you think it will make your life more interesting. Know how to find excitement in healthy things like sports, travel, music, or whatever hobbies you might have. But arguing with people on social media is not a hobby. Avoid drama in all of its forms, and you will be a happier person. This also means don't put pressure on yourself to be an "alpha male." Forget that and be a sheepdog. You'll be much happier, and you'll be much more useful to the world and to your community. Also, don't fear peace and quiet because you think it will be boring. Learn to be creative and have deep thoughts in those times of quiet. Don't be afraid to turn off the devices for a while and give yourself space to think and read. Read a real book. Read the Bible. And by the way, not only do real men read, but real men also write. Keep a journal and write down your thoughts, your dreams, your prayers, whatever. A man should have a place to write down what's important to him. Start right now by thinking about a few questions:

- Which of the fruit of the Spirit do you need to work on in your life?
- How do you define success?
- What kind of lifestyle do you hope to have?
- What would it look like for you to be a sheepdog?
- How has suffering or hardship in your life made you re-think what's important in life?
- What do you think of when you think of peace?
- What does peace of mind mean to you?
- What would peace and quiet look like in your life?
- What makes you happy?

THE MAN IN THE MIRROR

Well Gentlemen, I hope you have enjoyed this journey. This is far from the end; this is the beginning for all of you. I hope that, if you didn't take something away from every chapter, that you walk away from this book with at least one thing that will help you face the man in the mirror. As you stand there, I hope that you see that there is a little boy staring back at you, wanting you to never give up on your dreams. He is your compass. Your core. Your root. He is there wanting you to be well, healed, and whole. For, whoever you were born to be, it is never too late to become.

These 12 men (13, including my uncle) have shared a glimpse into their lives—their experiences, disappointments, and rewards. They have even shared some spaces where they still don't have the answers. But it is my hope for them, and all of you, that together you all will be able to see, embrace, and celebrate the little boy that lives inside of you.I salute you!

Jaime A. Gill

Ms. Jaime A. Gill is a certified life coach, author and self-reflection enthusiast. She is a sought-after speaker that leads workshops on personal development and leadership. She strives to deliver a message that will activate others to live their best life NOW.

Jaime is the author of *Lessons for The Little Girl* and *Lessons for The Little Boy.* This series is her hope to encourage women and men to willingly risk introspection for transformation and elevation. Her work as an author has been featured on WGN and Channel 26—WCIU, Chicago.

Through her presence in the compilation book *Sisterhood: Journeys of Women in Entrepreneurship,* Ms. Gill provides perspective in the power of pursuing your unique path to entrepreneurship.

With over 25 years of media experience, Jaime has produced content for local and international broadcasts including where she began as an intern, NBC—Chicago. She has been honored to produce for The American Cancer Society, History Makers, The Illinois Black Hall of Fame, Celebrity Financial Coach Lynn Richardson, Media Mogul—Russell Simmons, and philanthropist and Music Legend, MC Lyte.

Through her Chicago based radio show *The L.O.V.E PERSPECTIVE* (Lives of Vision and Empowerment) Jaime and co-host Alicia Bowens shared guests and topics to help their national listeners to live on purpose, with purpose, and for purpose. For her commitment to excellence in Media and technology, Ms. Gill was recognized by the Top Ladies of Distinction—Lincoln Park Chicago Chapter with the Crown Jewel Award.

Ms. Gill believes that service is a necessary ingredient to a successful life. Once a victim, now a thriver, Jaime volunteers to empower other victims of sexual assault by partnering with organizations to shatter the silence and erase the ignorance of sexual violence. She was recognized by Jack and Jill of America, Inc. South Suburban Chapter for her efforts to educate communities and empower victims. She was also featured on the cover of The W.E.L.L. Magazine as she shares her story of survival to triumph.

Through her life and commitment to serving others, Jaime was recognized as one of the inaugural women to be recognized by the Chi Lambda Lambda Chapter of Omega Psi Phi, Fraternity Inc., as a Woman of Distinction. Her life of service began at a very early age and even awarded her the opportunity to be on first cover of Guidepost for *Teen Magazine* with a featured article on her annual commitment to the Angel Tree Program.

Jaime Gill currently resides in Daytona Beach, Florida where she enjoys a career in the emergency room as a consumer access specialist, providing quality service and support to patients and families in their most vulnerable times of life. Jaime's name in French literally translates "to love" which is what she hopes to project through her life's works.

For More Information about Jaime A. Gill:

Website: www.jaimeagill.com
Facebook, Instagram, Twitter, Snapchat, TikTok: @ jaimeagill

Glenn Murray is the founder of 220 Holdings, the parent company to 220 Publishing , 220 Media and Food Wine and Spirit Ventures. Through 220 Publishing, he has published more than 50 titles across all genres. As a writer, Glenn has blogged for the NBC Chicago Street Teams, contributed articles to 360 Magazine, authored the blog, *Stop, Look, Listen,* for *Chicagonow.com* and contributed to *The Entrepreneur Within You* book series. In 2019, he released his first solo work, *You Wrote It, Now Go Sell It, A Marketing and Promotions Guide for Authors in A Few Simple Steps.* He is a contributor to the best selling *Faith, Failure, Success : Stories Along the Entrepreneurial Journey.*

He co-founded film and television production entity G-Rose Productions. He's co-written four film scripts including one based on one of the 220 Publishing releases *Love Miscarriage* and two television series and co-produced the un-scripted series *Making Love Better Twogether* and *Live From the Cave* and *Books and Bottles* airing on Streaming Service Inde TV He has been featured in *Rolling Out, Ebony/Jet Online* and the *Chicago Sun Times, Voyage Atlanta Magazine,* and *The Backstory Television Show* . He was selected by The Chicago Defender as one of the "50 Men of Excellence" and Who's Who Black Chicago and Atlanta. He has been a frequent guest on the *Smart Marketing for Small Business Radio Show, Voices of Change, and the Live Exchange* Podcasts.

Find out more about Glenn Murray:

Facebook: https://www.facebook.com/glenn.murray.7798/
https://www.facebook.com/glenn220

Twitter: https://twitter.com/Glenn220

Instagram: https://www.instagram.com/glenn220/

YouTube: https://www.youtube.com/
playlist?list=PLad6ZXyzFUhnKIRVCp-PoHmzAynbOirEQ

https://www.youtube.com/channel/UCkgFQdpftUe_Hhx3zrMHUIw

Blog: http://www.chicagonow.com/stop-look-listen/

Amazon Author Page: https://www.amazon.com/
Glenn-R.-Murray/e/B01M4O81XE?ref_=dbs_p_pbk_r00_abau_000000

220 Publishing: www.220books.com

Jim Smith is a former professional football player. Smith was a standout flanker/wingback for the University of Michigan during the mid 1970s. A versatile, all-around threat. He had 73 receptions for 1,687 yards and 14 touchdowns during his career at Michigan He ended a marvelous college career with 35 consecutive starts, 4 varsity letters, 2 Big Ten Championships, and Big Ten and All-American honors.

Smith was drafted in the third round by the Pittsburgh Steelers in 1977 and went on to win two Super Bowls with the famed Steel Curtain team in 1978 and 1979. He played wide receiver for six seasons for the Pittsburgh Steelers of the National Football League before being wooed by the Birmingham Stallions to the newly formed United States Football League. He signed one of the richest contracts in that league's short history. When the league folded in 1985, Smith played one more season in the NFL with the Los Angeles Raiders before beginning a 32-year career in the automobile industry.

He is a deeply devoted family man that enjoys spending time with his family.

Willow James is a theatre artist and photographer from the Chicago-land area, who works to instill his passion for kindness and celebrating blackness into his work. He is currently the resident sound designer at Artemisia Theatre and co-produces their *We Women Podcast.* He also co-produces/hosts a podcast called "That's What We Read: A Bookcast," and is proudly represented by Chicago Talent Network.

Find out more about Willow at:

Website: willow-james.org
Instagram: @worksbywillow

Freddie B. Arnold, Jr. is a Construction Manager with expertise in architecture, construction management, and restaurant development. Freddie worked with McDonald's Corporation in Operations for 10 years overseeing restaurant operations in both Illinois and Indiana before leaving in 2004 to focus strictly on architecture and construction. In 2004 he joined the George Sollitt Construction Company.

The past 16 years Freddie has been involved in the oversight, analysis and construction of over $1B in projects, ranging from Healthcare, Education, Religion, Multi-Unit Housing and Government agencies. In 2018, he was named "Estimator of the Year" by the Association of Subcontractors and Affiliates General Contractors Council. In 2020, Freddie was the recipient of Chicago Defender's Men of Excellence Class of 2020 Awards, which recognizes 50 world-class men from the Chicagoland area who have displayed the highest level of leadership. He holds a Bachelors in Architecture from the University of IL-Chicago and a Masters in Construction Engineering and Management from the Illinois Institute of Technology.

Freddie is Elder at Pullman Presbyterian Church, a mentor for YOUNG M.I.N.D.S., a member of Free & Accepted Masons (P.H.A.) and Immediate Past Basileus of Omega Psi Phi Fraternity, Inc., Chi Lambda Lambda Chapter. He resides in South Holland, IL with his wife of 25 years, Valicienne and daughters; Adrienne, Kennedy and Autumn.

Find out more about Freddie B. Arnold, Jr.:

Facebook: https://www.facebook.com/fred.arnold.5688/
Instagram: https://www.instagram.com/hqmmerque/
Interview: https://www.facebook.com
/beansouptimes/videos/10160225248450184

For nearly a quarter of a century, Bishop Kevin has been serving in the Ministry in various capacities. Whitaker is the former pastor of the Historical Mt. Pisgah Baptist Church. He and his wife founded and led Raising the Standard International Ministries for eleven years and are currently the pastors and founders of Epic Church Atlanta International located in Douglasville, Georgia. Over the years, Bishop Whitaker has hosted his own radio show on 1600 AM in Memphis, Tennessee as well as hosted his very own telecast on Good News TV. He has been featured on TBN, TV 57 in Atlanta, Majesty Now Network in Waycross Georgia, as well as on the Word Network. Bishop Kevin Whitaker is also noted for publishing his first book, *2 Hard 2 Break,* in 2015. This book allotted him several opportunities to share his personal deliverance story and truly define the idea of turning one's life around. Because of this book, his reach expanded beyond Christian platforms into secular radio programs as well. During this time, he was also a guest panelist at DePaul University and he has become a valuable contributor to several other books.

Bishop Whitaker has been instrumental in partnering with the Girls and Boys Club of America to have peace rallies; including the head of the gang unit, the District Attorney, and also former gang leaders. He has worked diligently in the school system doing gang intervention with troubled youth providing guidance and motivation to complete school and prayerfully attend college.

In 2017, Apostle Kevin Whitaker was duly consecrated into the office of

Bishop with Apostolic Succession and is a member of the joint college of African American Bishops. As an Apostle, he serves as a gift to the body traveling nationally and abroad to preach the gospel. The mantle on his life invigorates those around him to be the best they can be. He serves as a Mentor and Spiritual Father to other pastors providing Apostolic covering and is considered by many as a true servant leader. He holds a degree in Electronic Engineering and Certified Master Chaplain.

Bishop Whitaker has accomplished great things, and the greatest above all is being married to his wife for twenty years and being the father of five daughters.

Find out more about Kevin Whitatker:

Facebook: @KEVIN WHITAKER
Instagram: @BISHOP_KWHITAKER
Twitter: @APREACHA

Peyton Rose is an award-winning author, Spartan athlete, husband, father, and Founder of Alpha Wave, LLC. He believes anything is possible for people when they put their minds to the task. His mission is to help folks optimize their daily lives and reach their full potential by changing mindsets and creating small habits that have huge impacts.

I am so proud to share a snapshot of all I've learned on my journey.

Find out more about Peyton Rose:

Website: alphawavegroup.com

Email: peyton@alphawavegroup.com

Instagram: @peytonrose34

Shawn Mason is a Chicago based Artist and Entrepreneur. After having created a local following as a singer/songwriter, Shawn transitioned his love for writing lyrics to writing prose, poetry and eventually a weekly blog. His love for meaningful dialog led to him being noticed by part of the production team at Inde.tv, an independent streaming network in Chicago. Ultimately, he was selected to host the network's popular show *Live From The Cave.* In June 2012 Shawn launched Evan Marcus Imagery, which is now a full service photography operation.

When Shawn is not shooting, responding to a request to perform or preparing for the next episode of *Live From The Cave,* he can be found binge watching tv shows, enjoying movies or watching football while enjoying a self-made Old Fashioned or one of his favorite bourbons over ice with ginger beer.

Currently, Shawn is working on a number of book projects including a photography coffee table book and a romance novel.

Find out more about Shawn Mason:

Facebook: shawnmasonemi
        evanmarcusimagery
        MASON-138800984171

Instagram: @itsthecrooner
        @evanmarcusimagery

Eric Hampton and Jennifer, his beautiful wife, love raising their amazing sons, Ethan and Jacob, in the Chicago-land area.

Eric is also a church planter who understands the importance of God, family, community and culture.

With several years of experience serving as a founding senior pastor and executive pastor, Eric is also a ministry consultant for pastors, leaders, and churches. He also enjoys being a leadership podcast host that reaches and coaches spiritual and secular audiences.

Gifted in preaching, leadership, and administration, Eric has also earned a formal, graduate level education, and has earned certifications in Church Administration, Leadership, Nonprofit Management, Organizational Development, and Nonprofit Governance.

Eric has a sincere passion for the work of the church, not simply church work.

Find out more about Eric Hampton:

Website: www.ericvhampton.com

Evan Marc...

Anatomy of a Creative.

As a music industry veteran of more than 25 years, Kenery Kent Smith is part of a rich tradition of World Class Chicago bassists. His performance resume showcases the Chi-Town musical trademarks of extraordinary talent, and a versatility to work in any musical genre. Kenery's experience includes performances with artists ranging from international Neo Soul recording artist Erykah Badu, to world renowned Jazz vocal diva Dee Alexander. Kenery has provided low end grooves for Acid Jazz pioneers Liquid Soul, and he has laid down a funky groove or two behind world famous comedian Bernie Mac. And he has toured extensively throughout Italy, Germany, Switzerland and Luxembourg with the inspirational voices of Sue Conway and the Victory Singers, and with Pierre Walker & Project: Sanctified. Kenery has also performed locally with Gospel legend Kim Stratton, Grammy winning recording artist Darius Brooks, Gospel recording artist Phil Tarver.

Kenery has worked in many other diverse musical settings including performing music with the world-renowned tap dance ensemble MADD Rhythms, touring nationally with Jackie Taylor's Black Ensemble Theater, and with Chicago's Free Street Theater (most notably at The Kennedy Center in Washington D.C.). Most recently, Kenery appeared in, and wrote and produced original music for the independent film *The Rise and Fall of Miss Thang*. And for 15 years Kenery was co-founder and bassist of Chicago's very own Nu-Jazz legends Detour JazFunk, with whom he shares writing, arranging, and co-production credits on their debut CD entitled *JazFunk*. Kenery can currently be seen and heard each week in the role of first chair bassist on the syndicated weekly Sunday morning broadcast of Victory Apostolic Church in Matteson IL., as part of their extraordinary music ministry.

Whether Kenery is writing music, lyrics... poetry or prose; the heart and mind of this Creative will always speak its truths in the most authentic, unique...and unapologetic manner. Because for Kenery, creativity through art is all about communication. It's all about expression. And it's all about sharing himself with the world, in order to answer the likely unasked question: who is Kenery Kent Smith? And his humble contribution to *Lessons For the Little Boy* gives you, the reader, a tiny peek into the process of answering that question.

Find out more about Kenery Kent Smith:

Website: www.K2SProductions.com

Facebook: musical.low.b
          k2sproductions/

Instagram: @W2kenerysmith

Lionel Hilaire is a husband, father of 3 girls and 1 son. Author of two books, *How To Rescue Yourself From Rescuing Others,* and *Cultivate Your Calling,* Speaker and the Treasurer of Divine Potential Services, Inc. which is a 501(c)(3) nonprofit organization whose mission is to restore families and empower change since 2016.

His ultimate purpose in life is to see lives properly positioned to prosper on purpose through marketing, consulting and coaching.

Lionel believes whole hardheartedly that self-discovery and cultivation is key to a fulfilled, effective and purposeful life.

Lionel enjoys playing basketball, bike riding, telling jokes and cooking with his family.

Writing this book helped me tap in a side of myself I thought would take years to reveal. The little boy with me is smiles today.

Find out more about Lionel Hilaire:

Website: www.LionelHilaire.com
Facebook and Instagram: @LionelHilaire

Mel Roberson is a six-time Amazon best selling author, accomplished actor, and dynamic speaker.

Born and raised on the south side of Chicago, Mel is the perfect blend of street smarts and book smarts. Mel was a victim of gun violence during his senior year of high school. That traumatic event changed his life, and propelled him forward. He has a B.S. in Political Science, post graduate studies in Integrated Marketing Communications, and dual MBAs in Management and HR. He has spoken in front of crowds from 5 to 15,000 delivering relatable personal and professional development talks for 15+ years.

At age 25, he was the youngest Regional Vice President for a NYSE traded company. He also has extensive entrepreneurial experience, starting and running four of his own companies. In addition to his business experience, Mel is an accomplished SAG actor (seen on *Chicago P.D.* On NBC, *The Chi* on Showtime Network, *Empire* on Fox, and many more) and an award-winning spoken word artist. He believes that his most important job is being a father to his two amazing daughters.

Find out more about Mel Roberson:
Website: www.melroberson.com

The Hazzard Group, LLC
Client focused... solution driven

Robert Hazzard is managing director of The Hazzard Group (THG), which is a boutique consulting firm dedicated to helping small and medium size companies solve their business problems with mobility solutions.

A technology nerd with a taste for solving business process problems, Robert skillfully connects the right mobile application to specific, even niche needs, allowing clients to realize efficiencies.

With skills honed over 17 years at AT&T and across multiple industries prior to that, Robert has shattered sales goals to the tune of 140%+ resulting in numerous circle of excellence award trips; created sales training programs for new hires; toured company circuits to speak on the importance of having a mobile strategy—proving his technical knowledge and leadership skills.

He brings to THG a broad and strategic approach with proven experience working with C-suite executives to transform their business. He is equally skilled at evaluating tactical lapses and working with team members closer to the front lines. This combined approach allows him to quickly assess a situation and determine the best solution.

Robert's office is in Chicago, IL but his reach and client base expands several major cities. Contact THG today, for a no-cost consultation and allow us to create a mobile solution designed to address your needs.

Find out more about Robert Hazzard:

Website: www.thehazzardgroup.com
Email: Robert@Thehazzardgroup.com

Carlo Kennedy is an Irish-Italian-American author known for the *Time Signature* novels. Carlo has traveled to all the places he writes about (except the past). He is an aficionado of traditional Irish music, and on occasion can be found performing Irish songs at Irish pubs. He is also a frequent presenter of workshops on creative writing and the writing process.

I'm honored to be able to contribute to this important book—a man has to be healthy in himself if he's going to have healthy relationships, and I'm blessed to have some small part in helping young men grow up healthy and happy.

Find out more about Carlo Kennedy:

Website: www.CarloKennedy.com

YouTube: www.CarloKennedy.net

For more information about the Time Signature novels:
www.TimeSignature.info